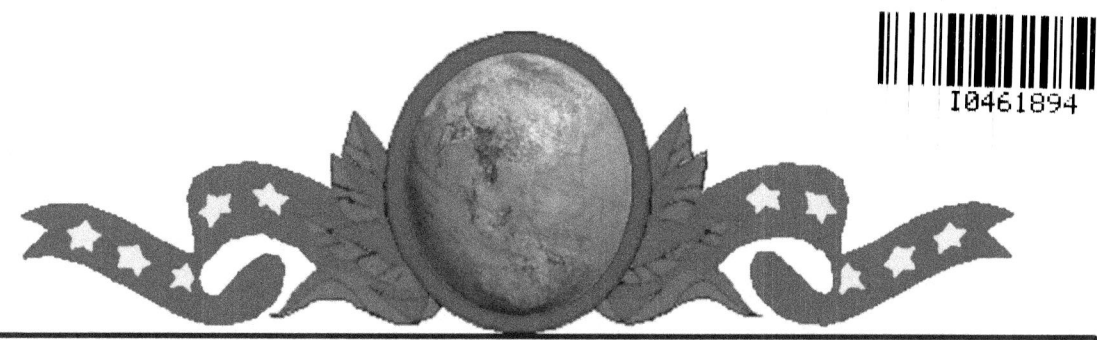

Real World
Colouring Book
For Advanced Users & Adults

Copyright 2019 By John Boom

50 Images

Created From Real Life Photos
For You To Colour As You Please.

ISBN 978-0-359-78855-2

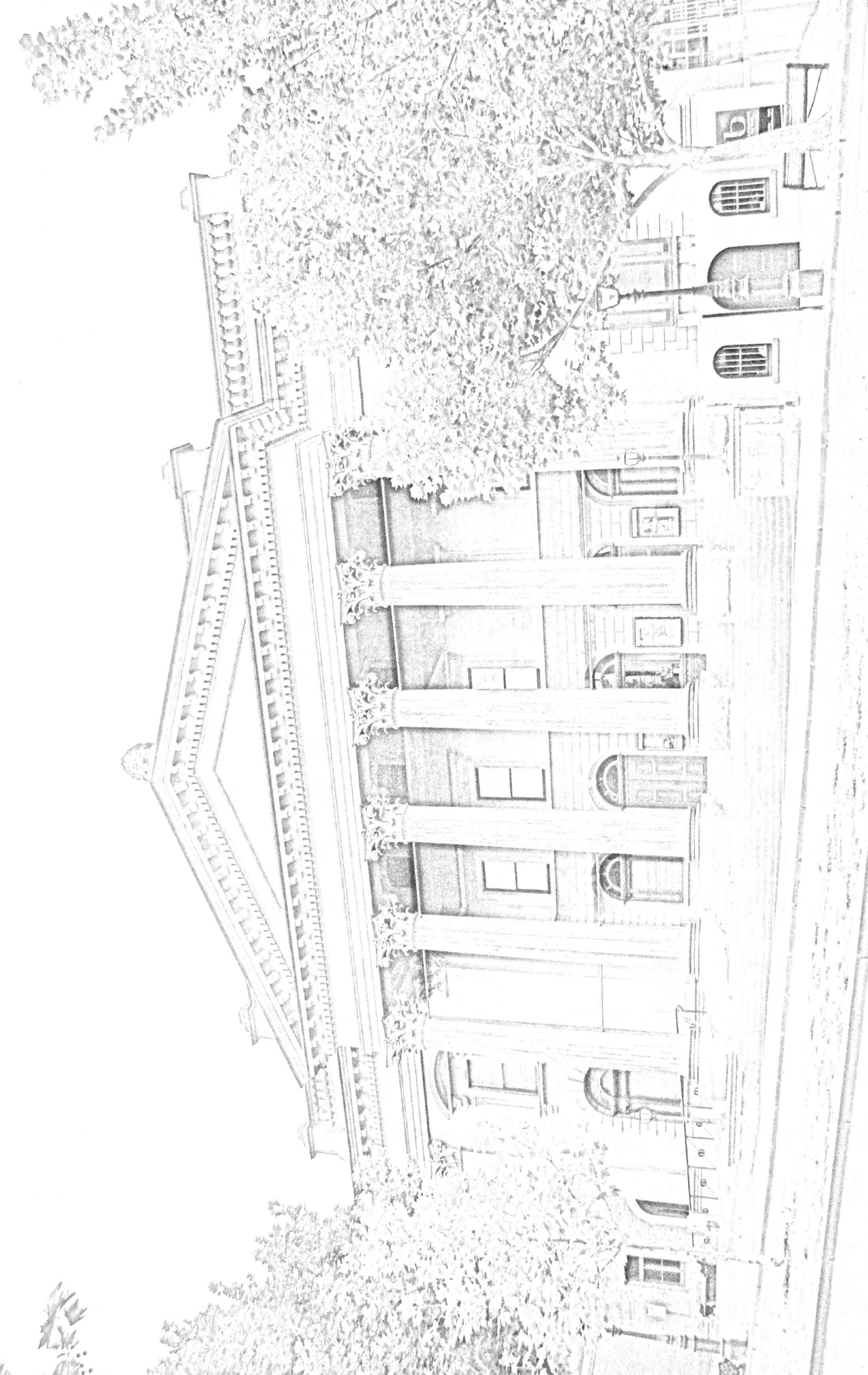

River Boat

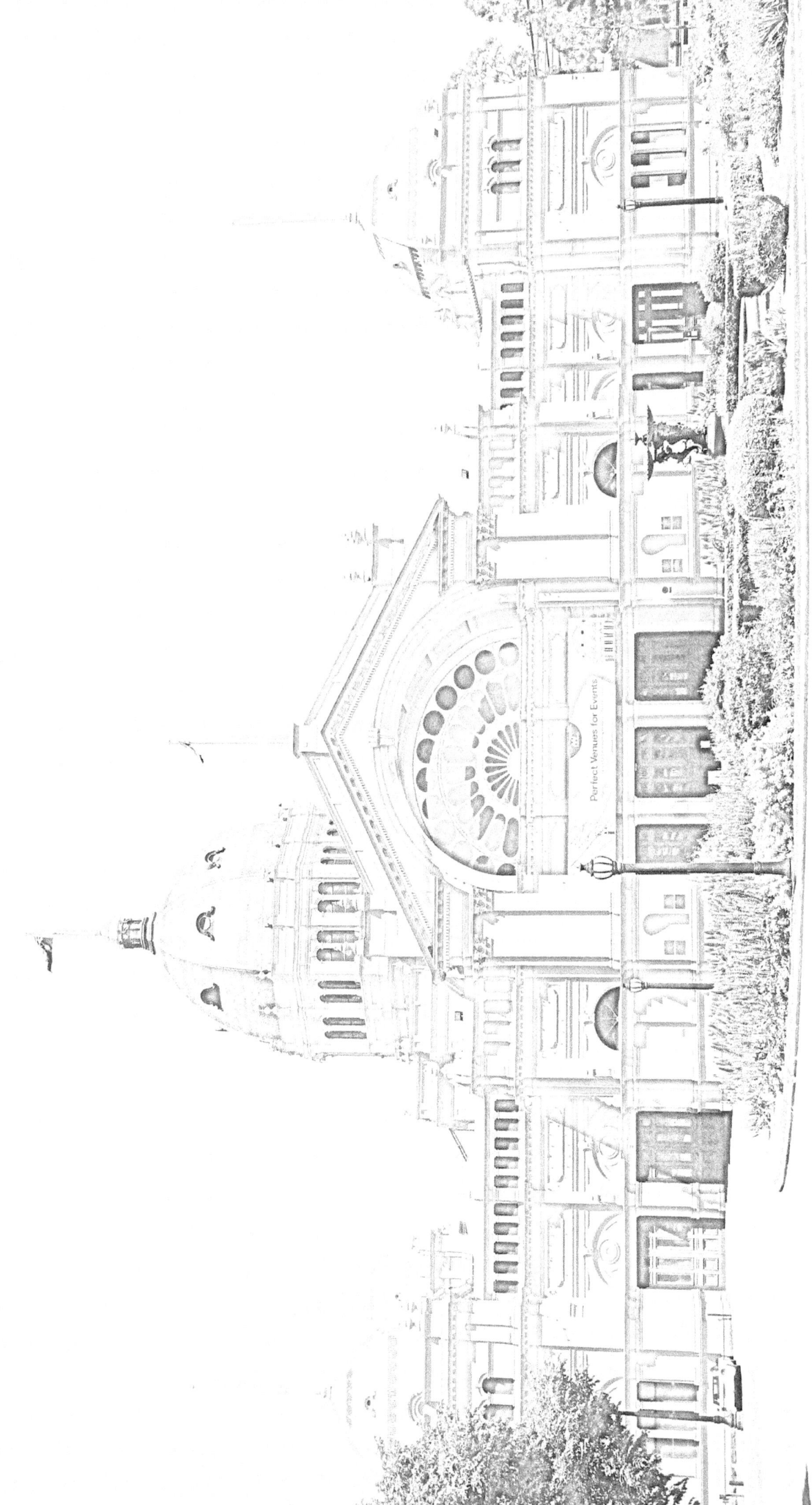

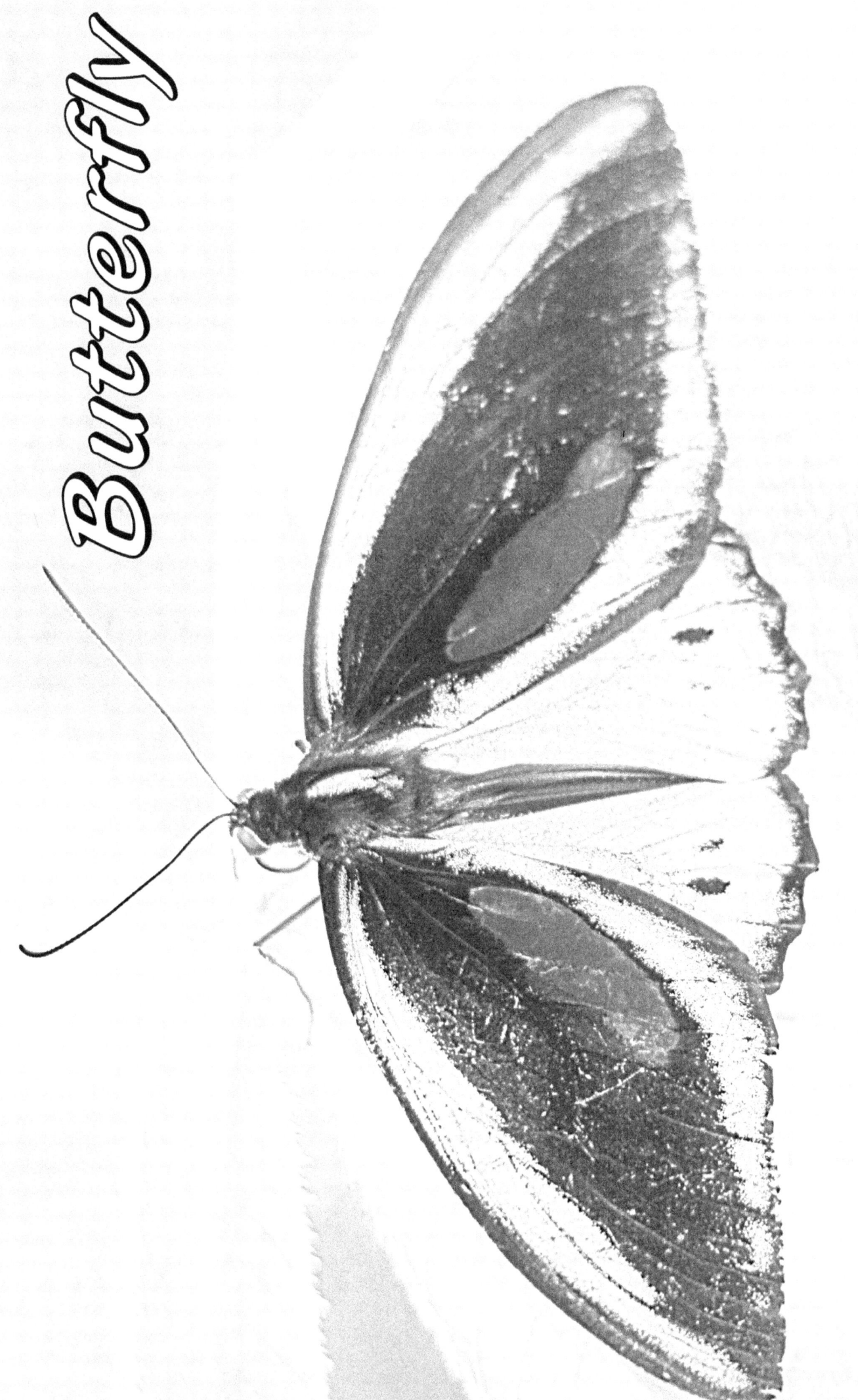

Butterfly

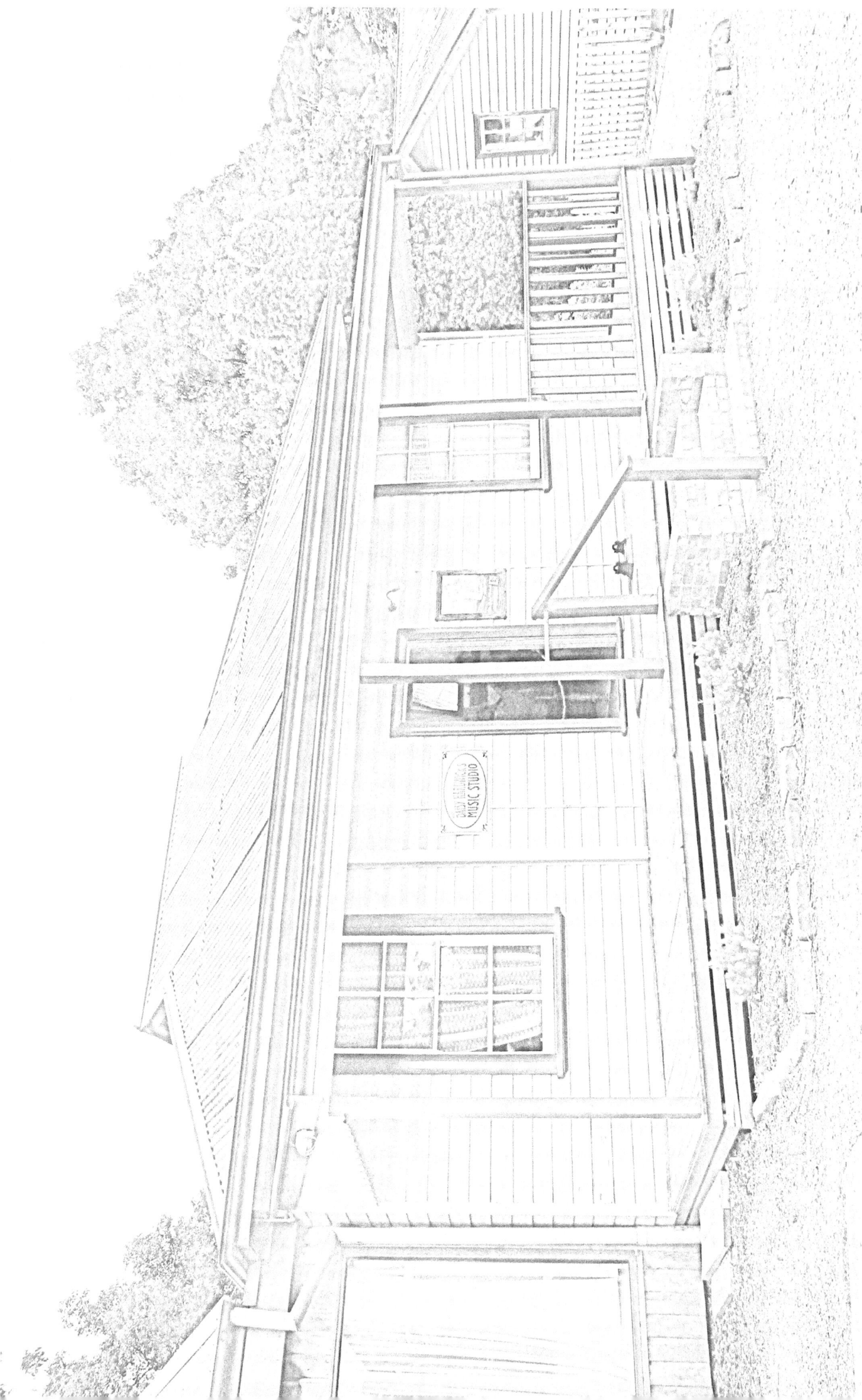

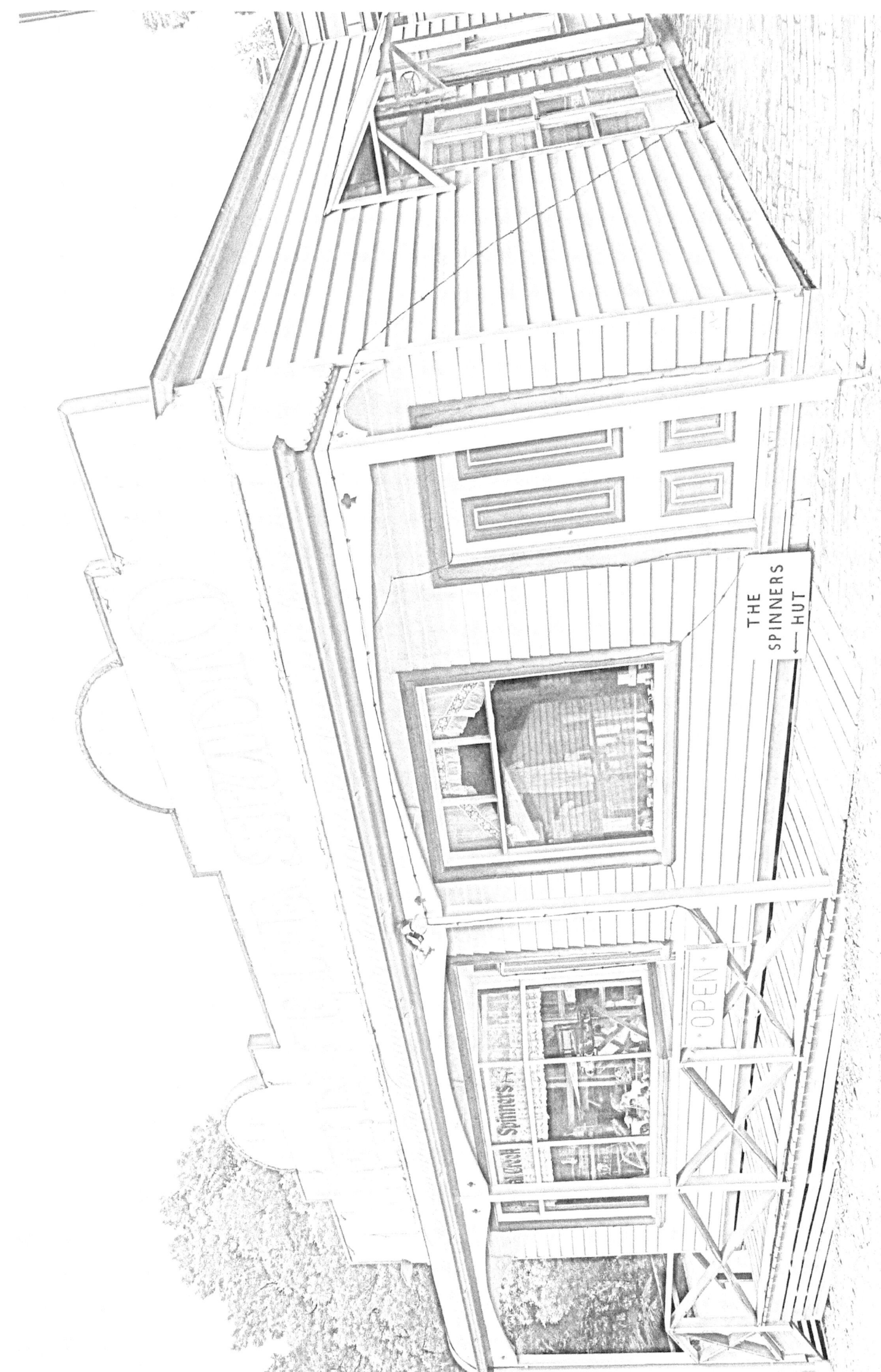

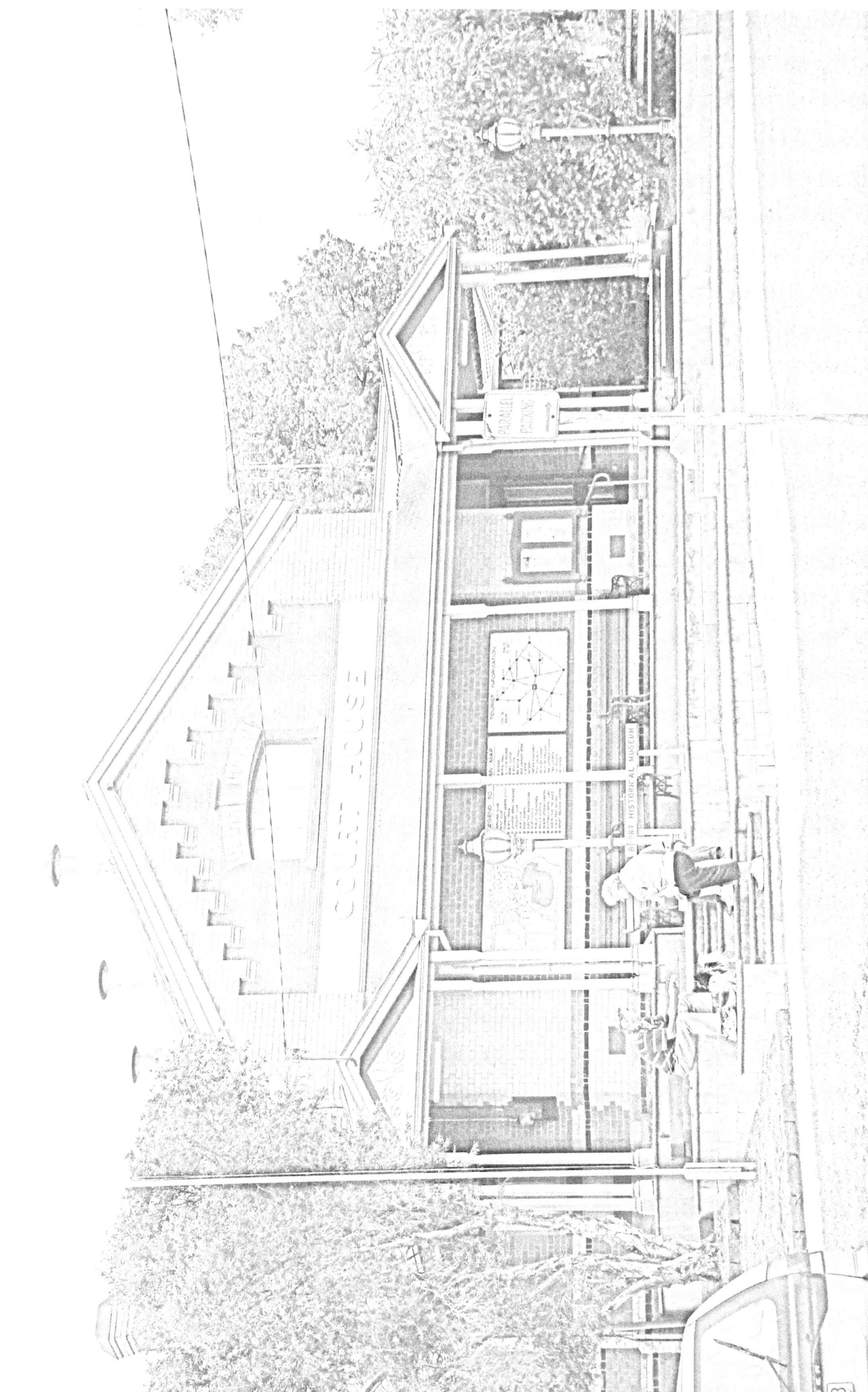

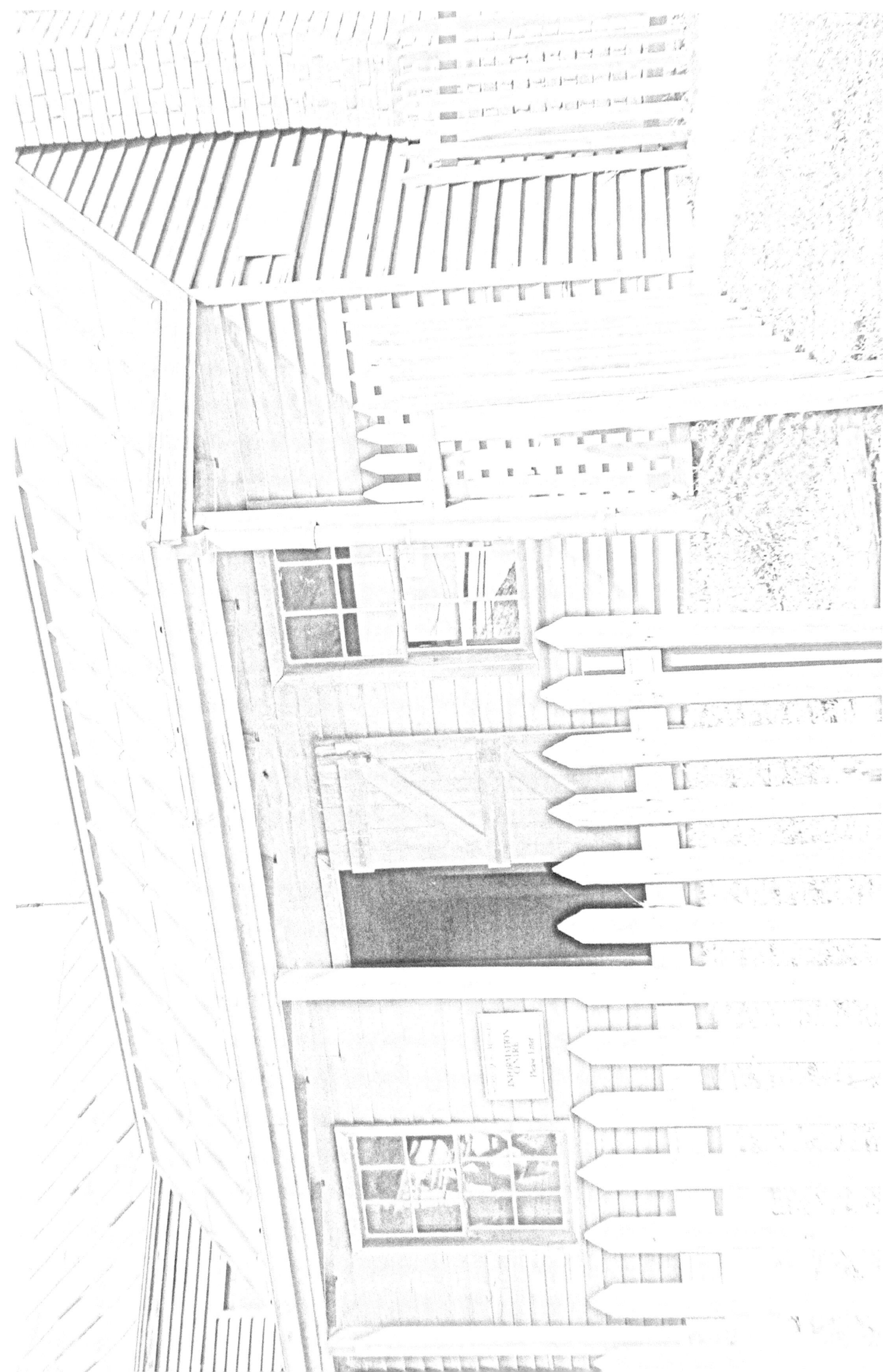

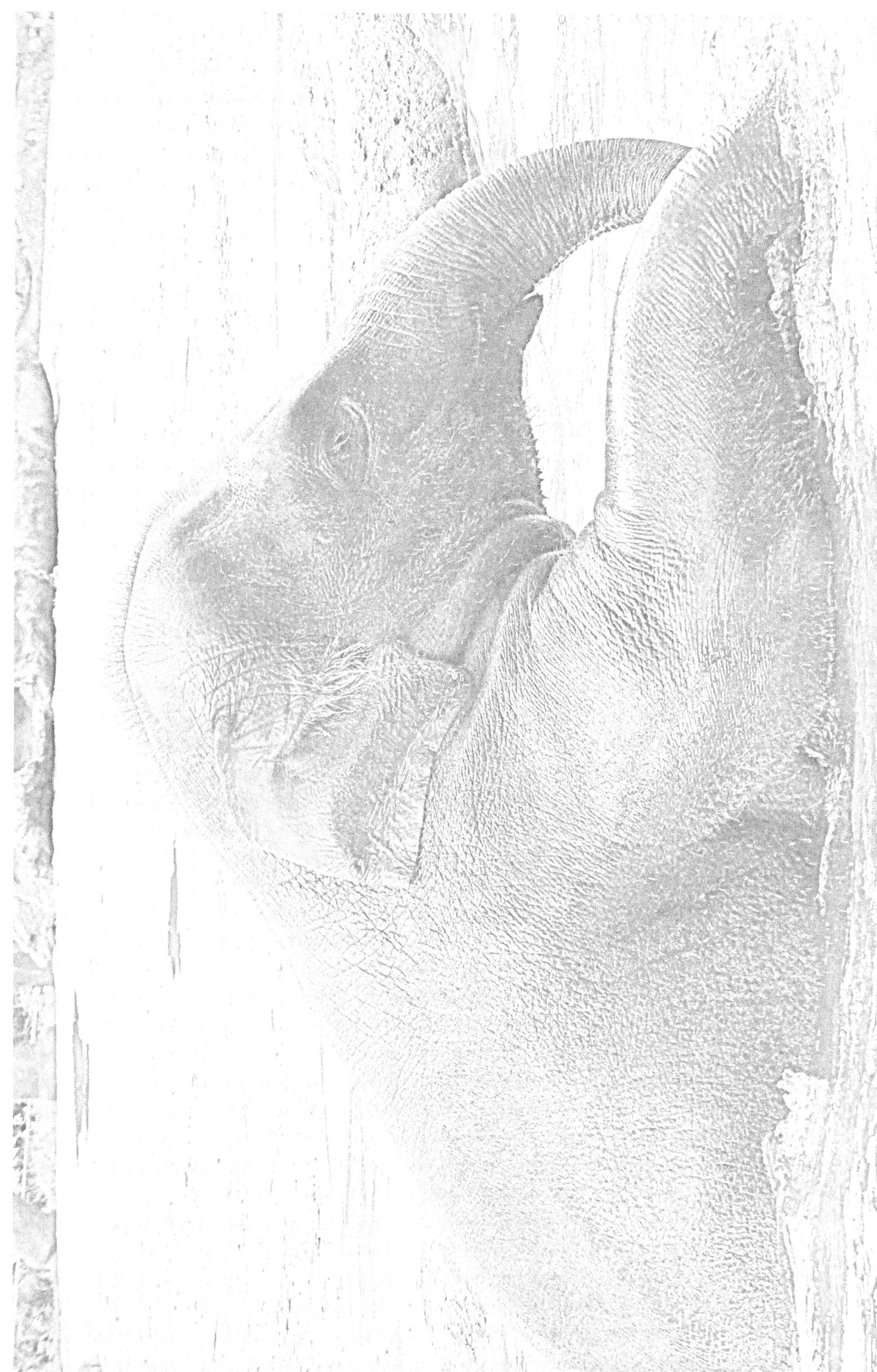

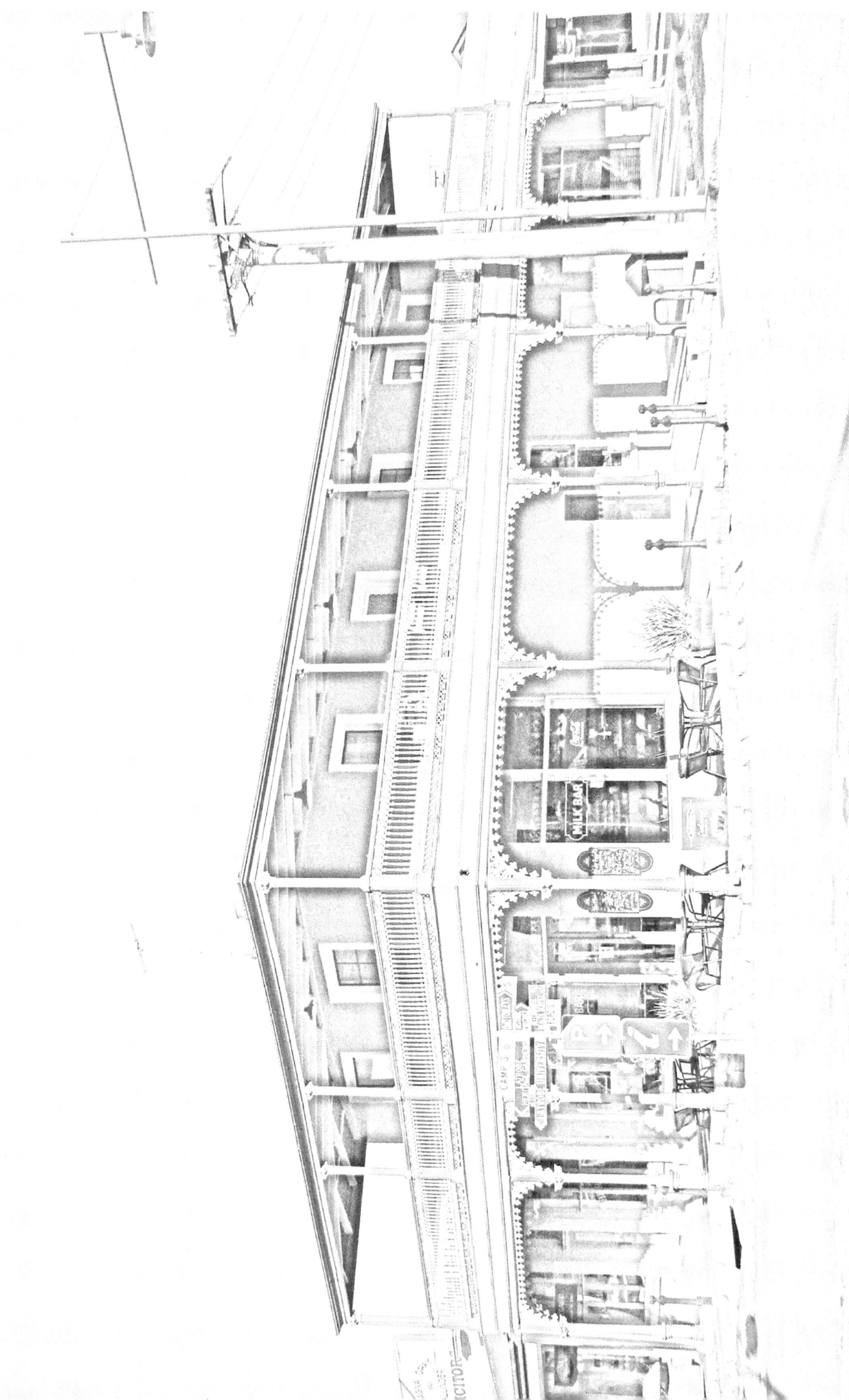

Hotel

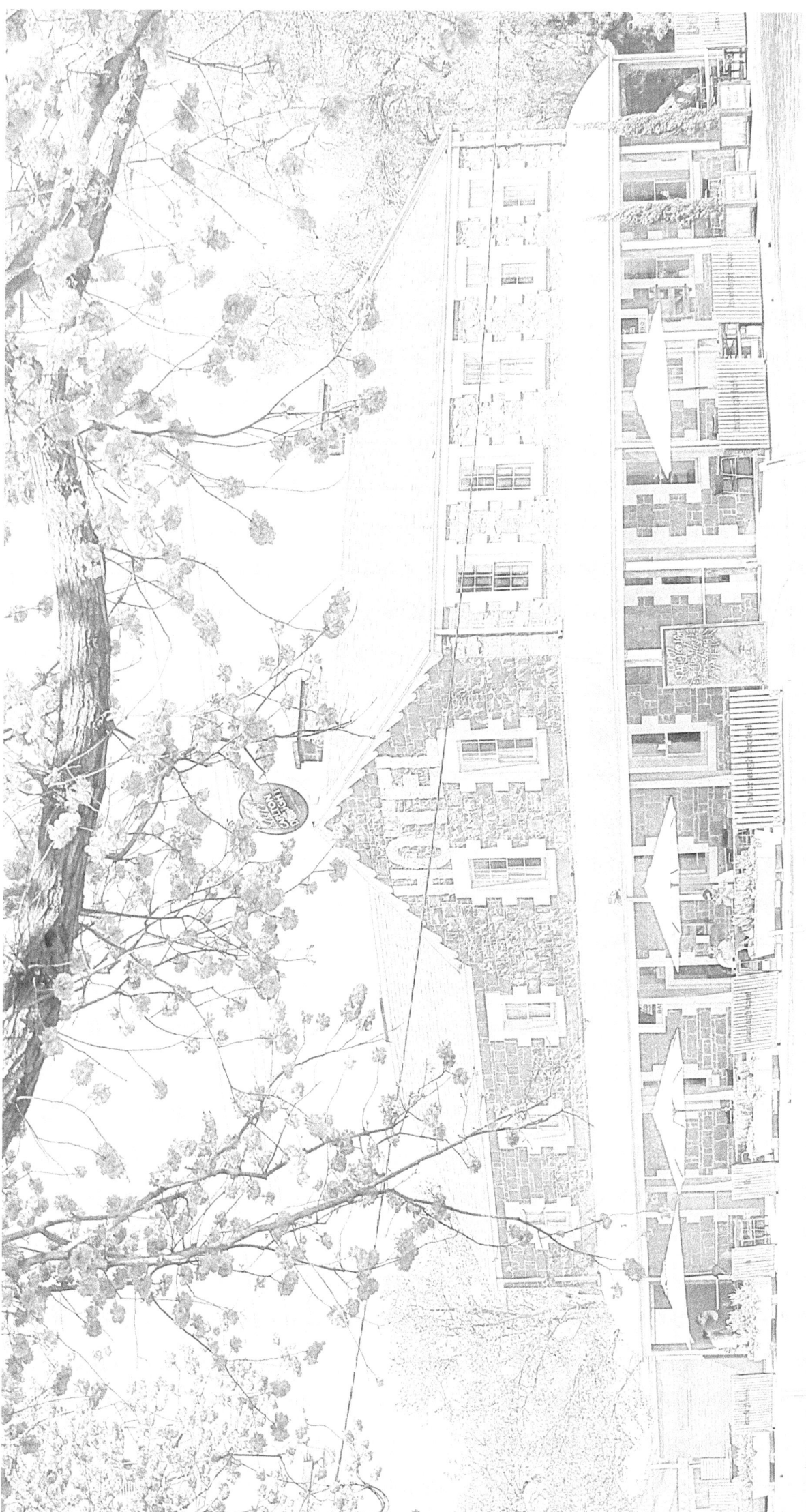

Hotel

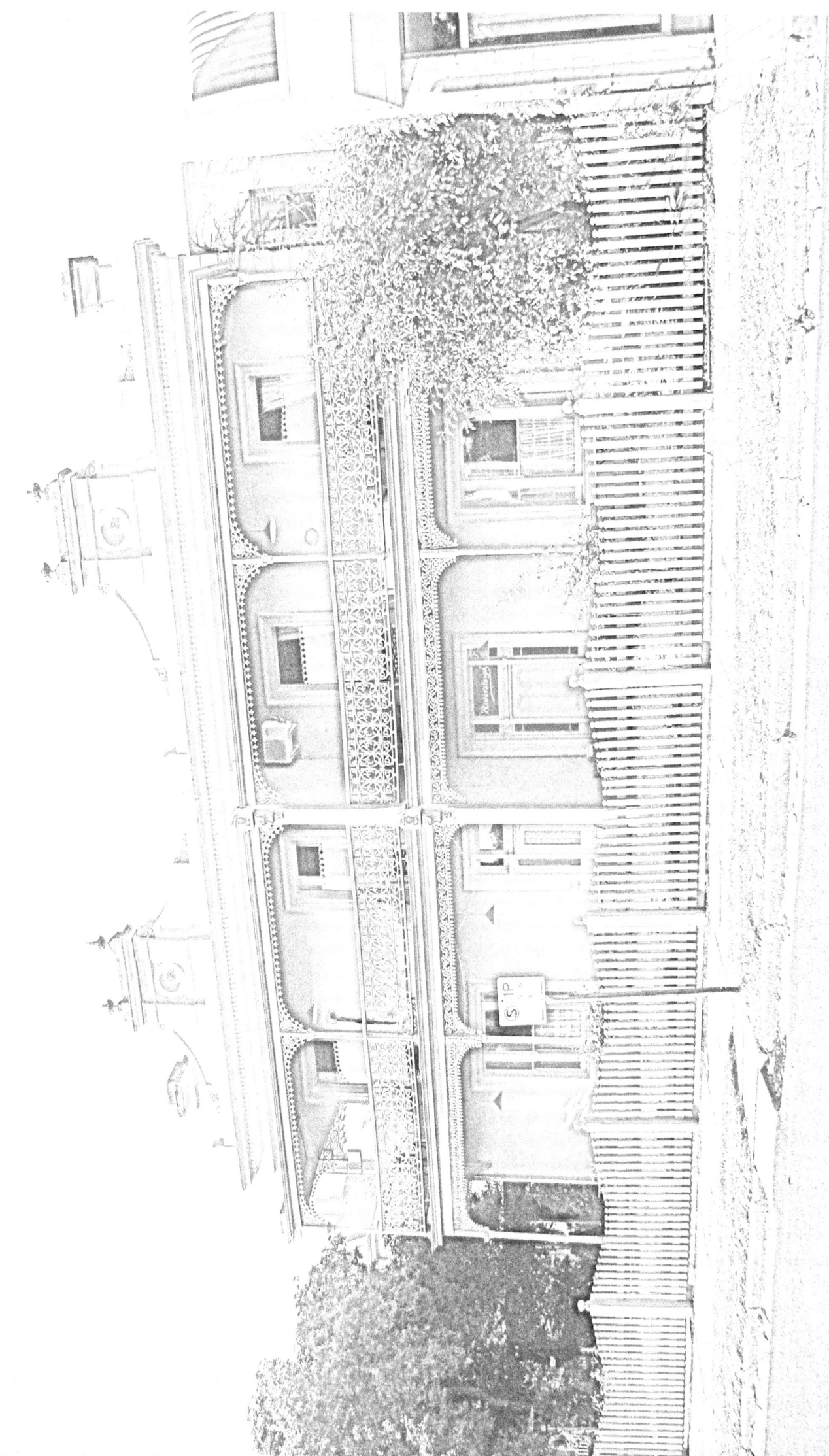

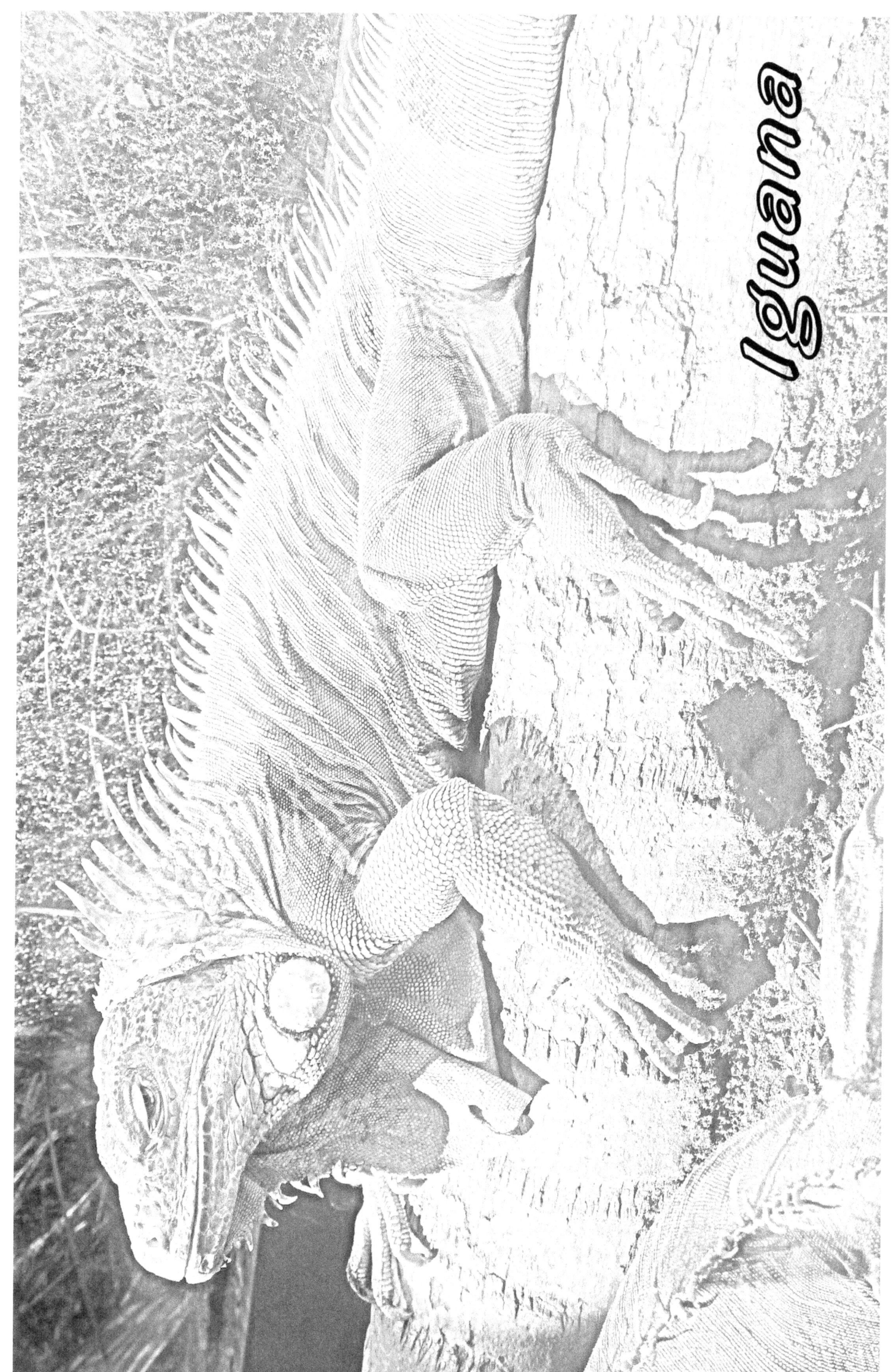

Iguana

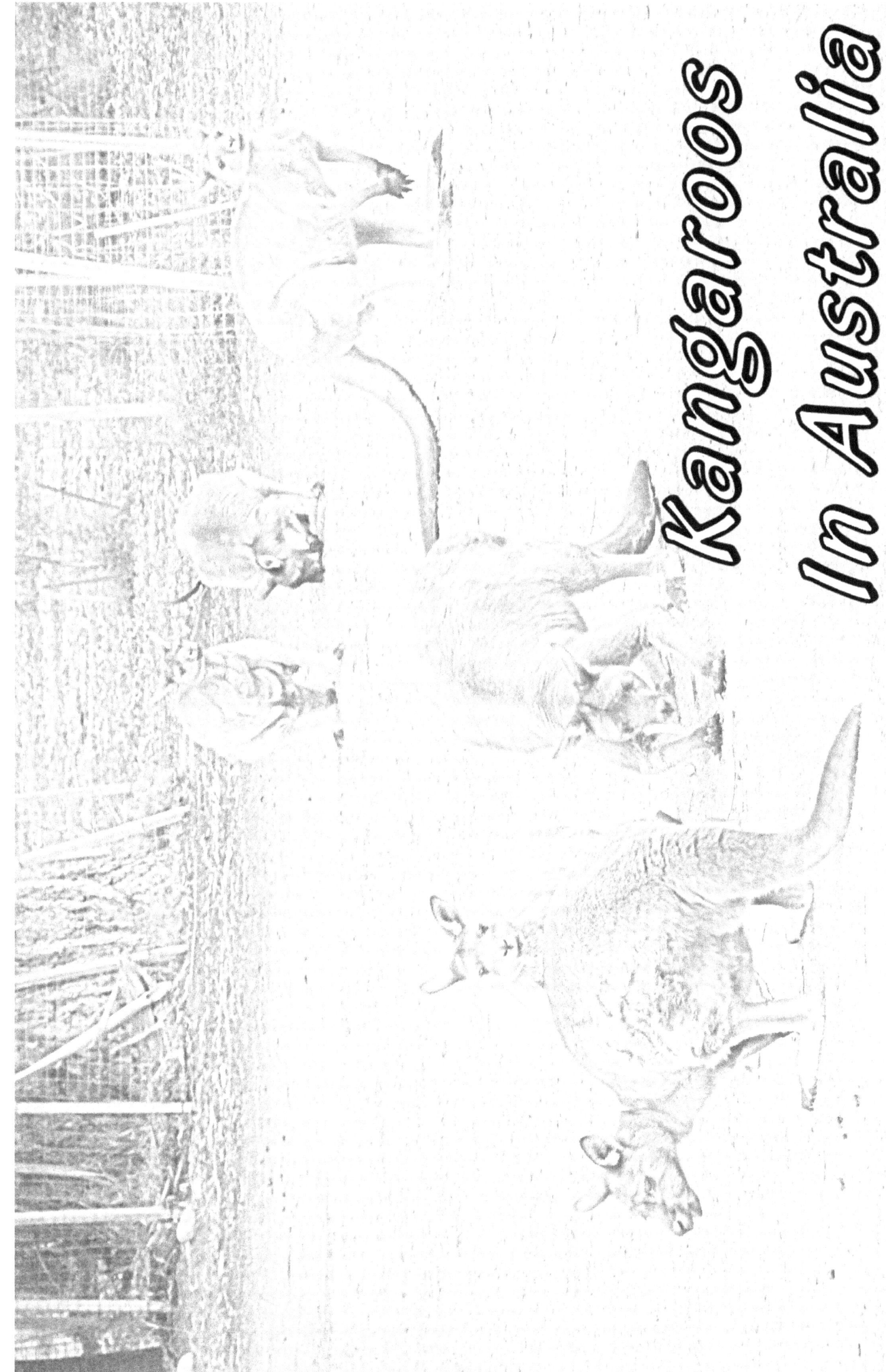

Kangaroos In Australia

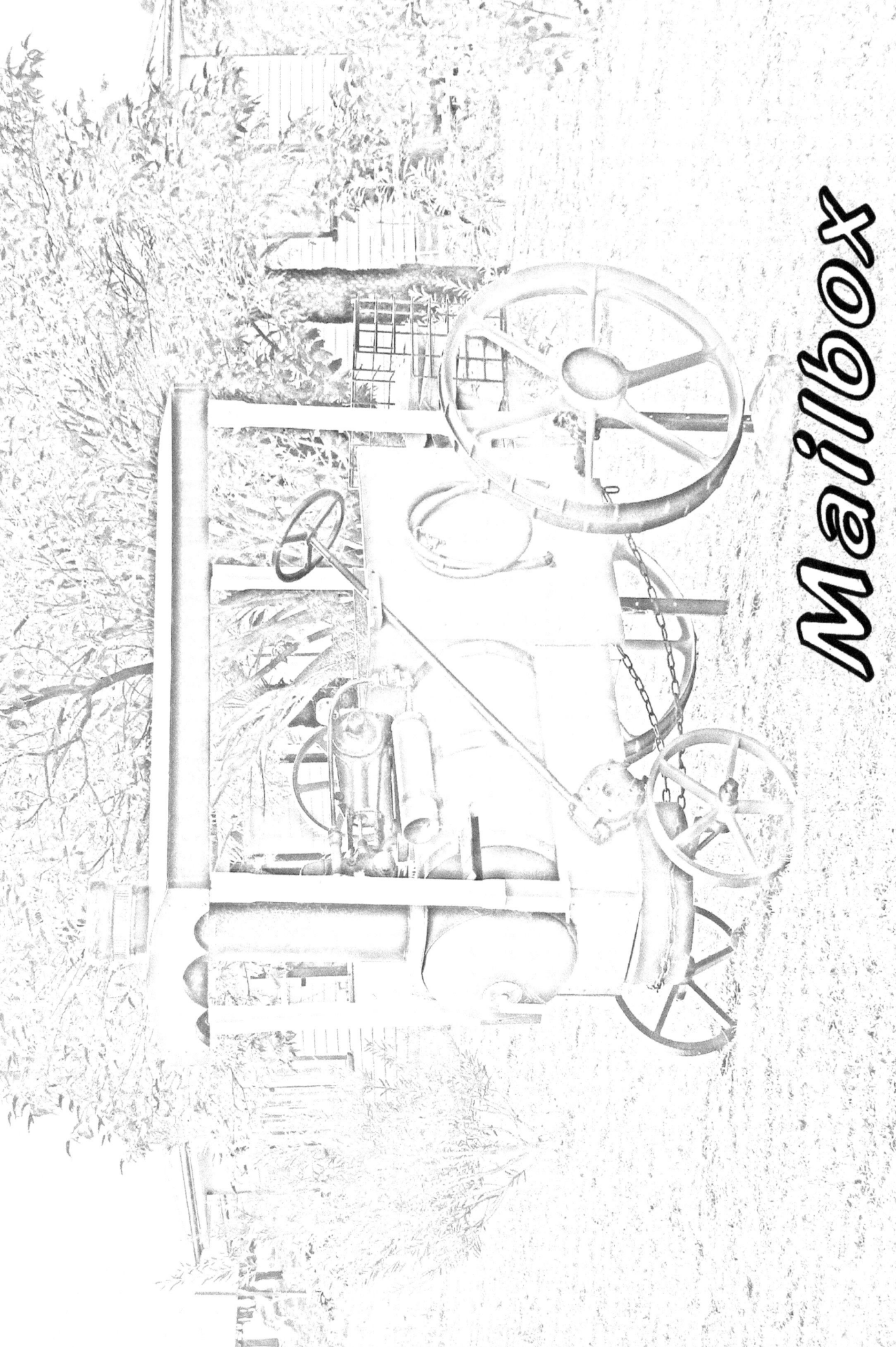

Mailbox

Museum

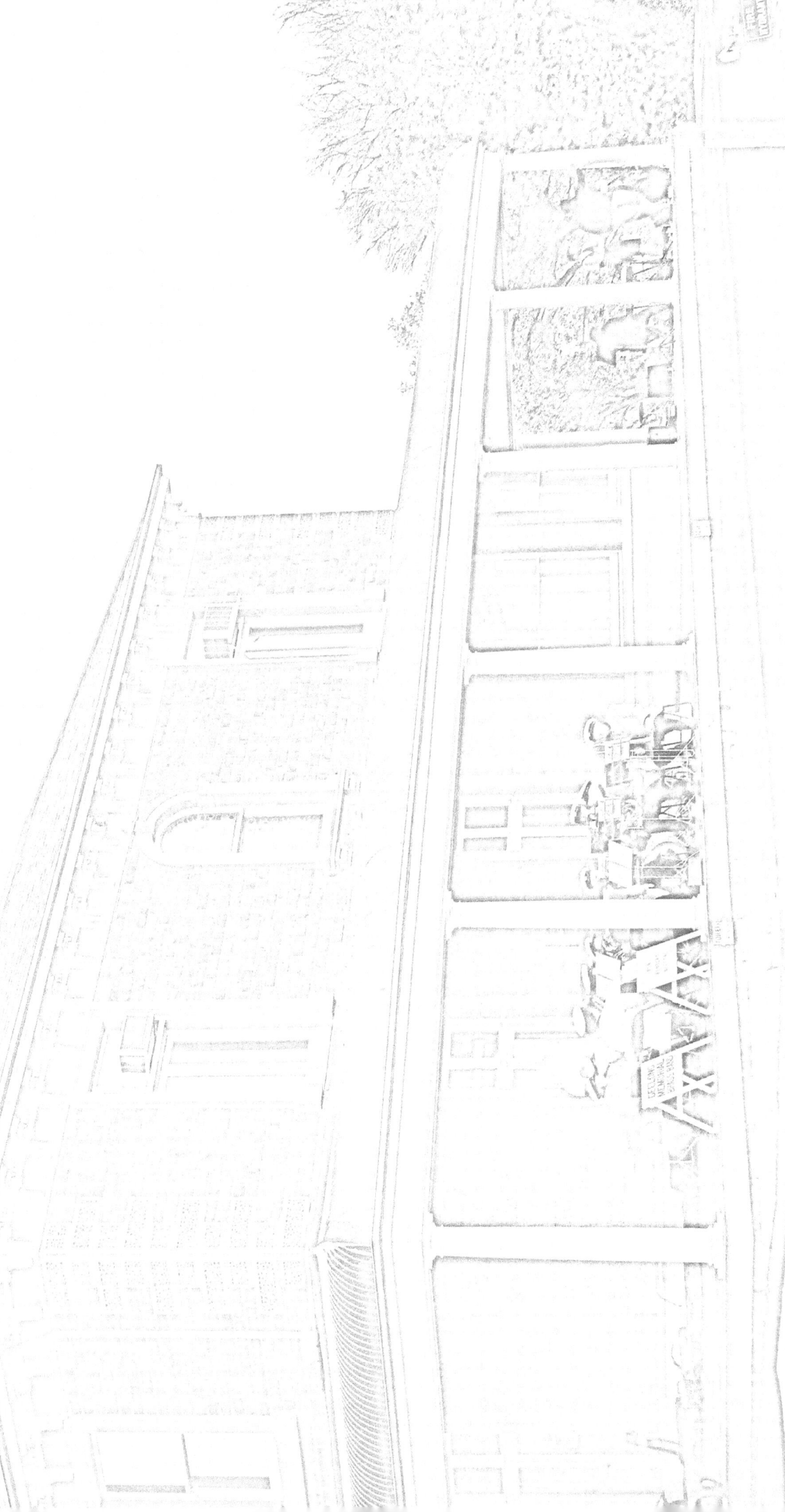

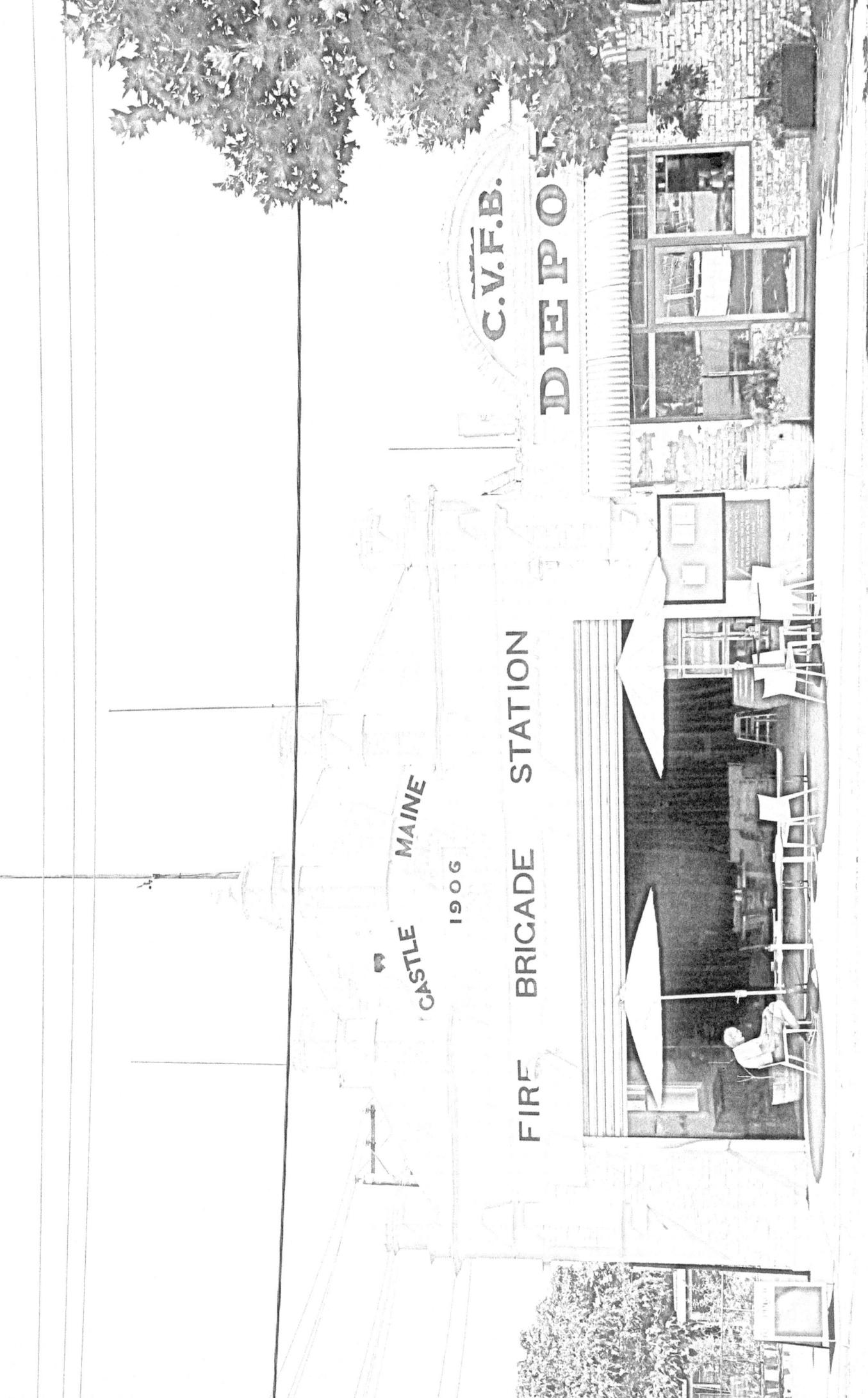

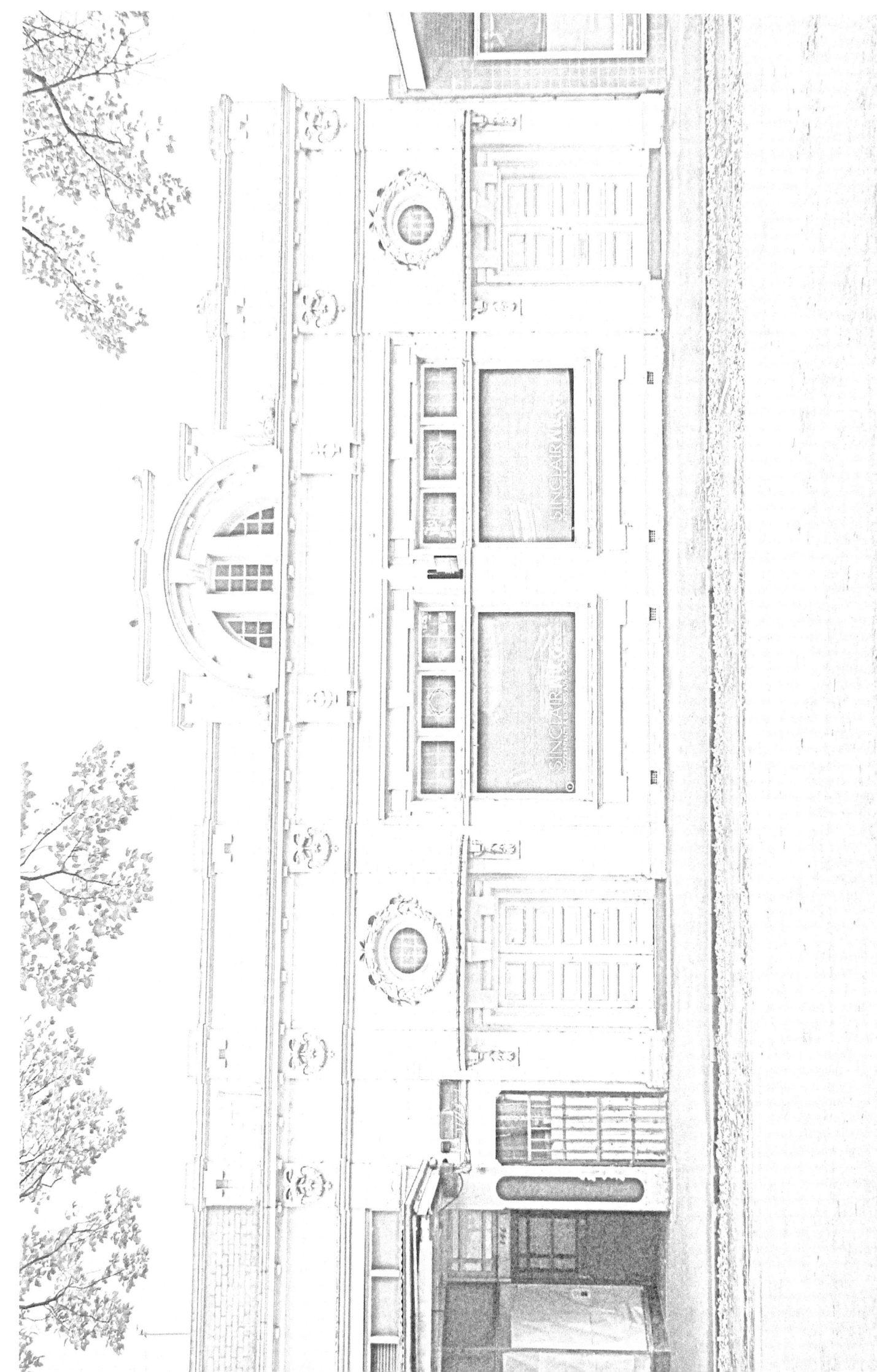

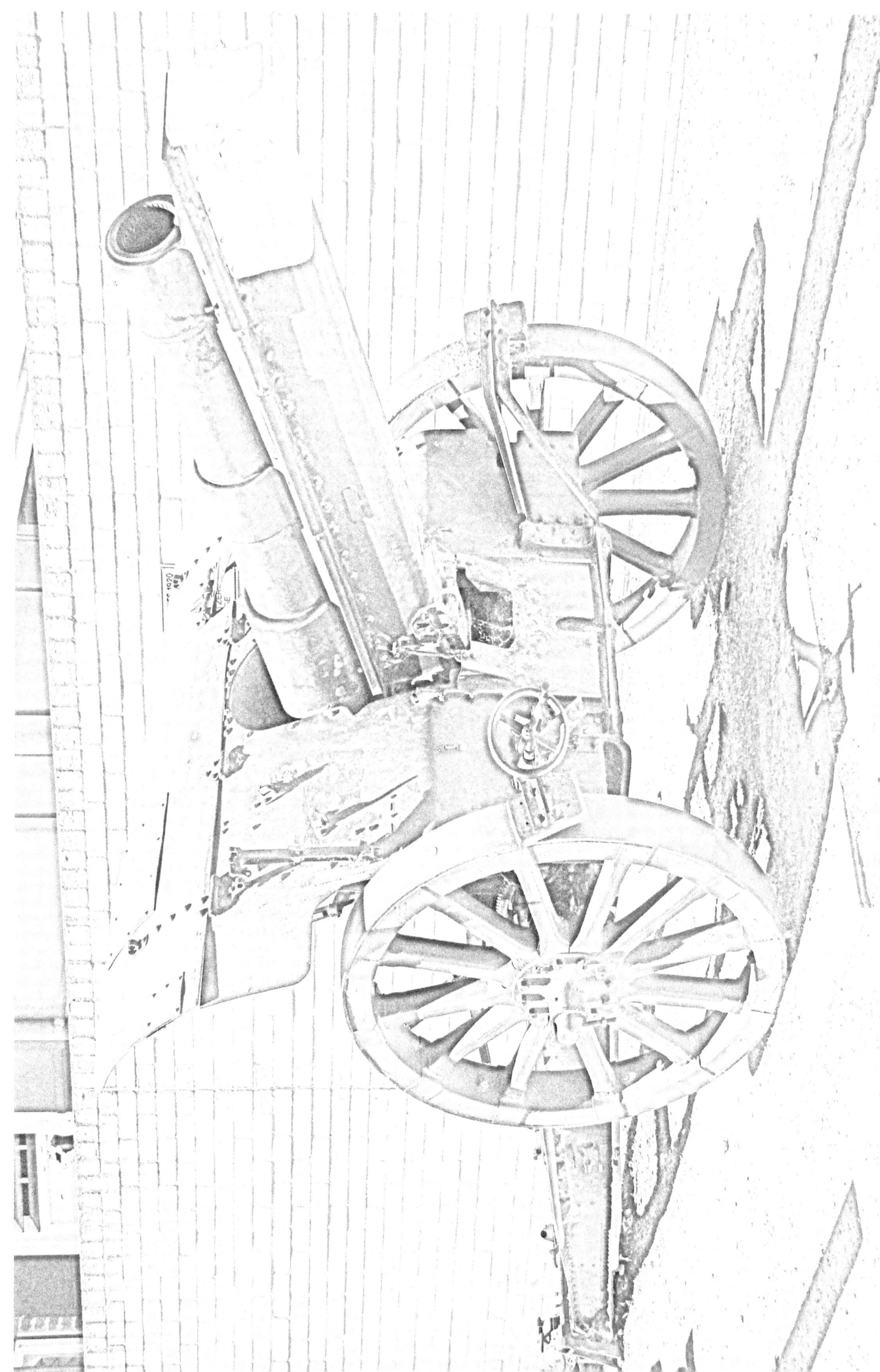

Roooster

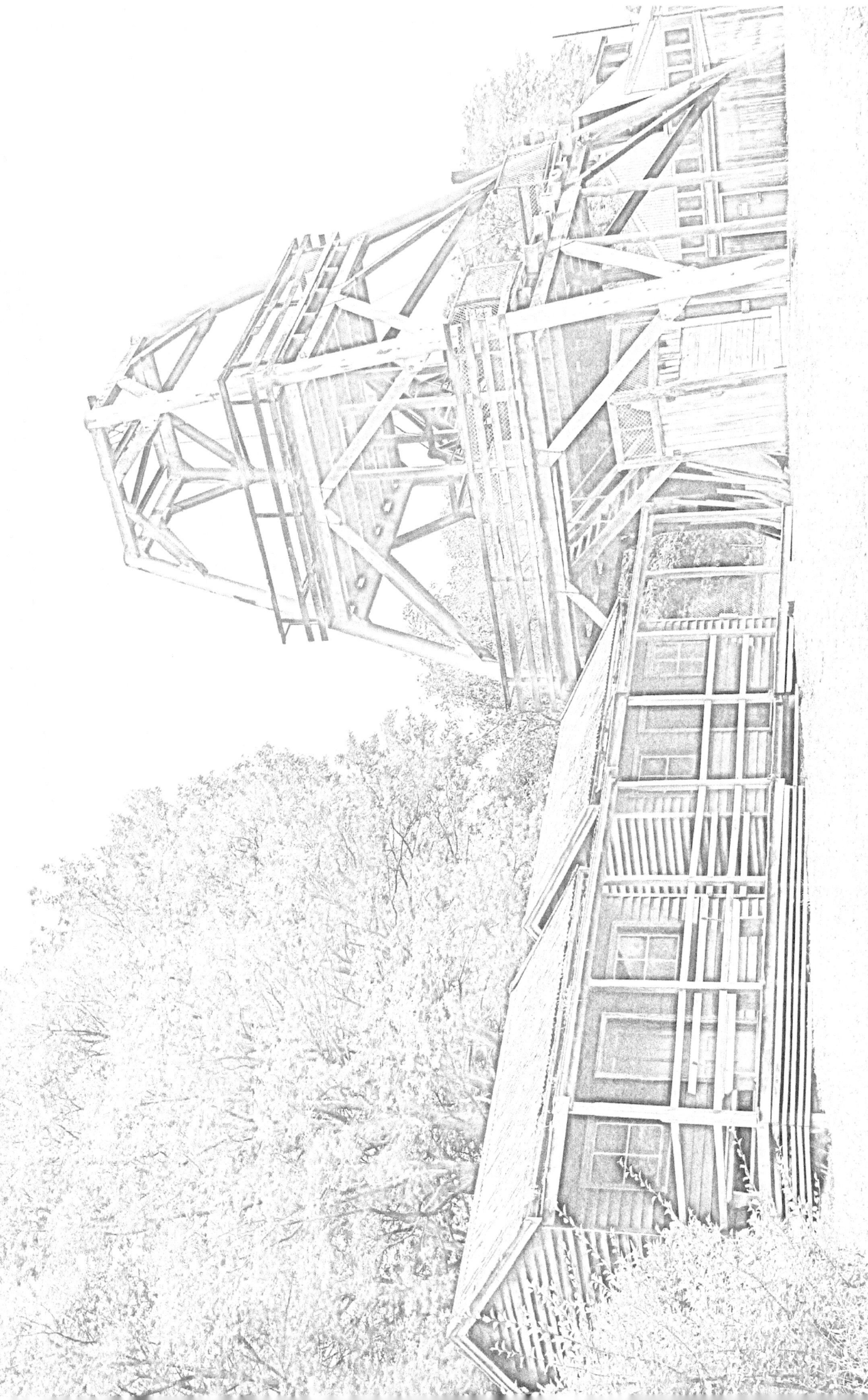

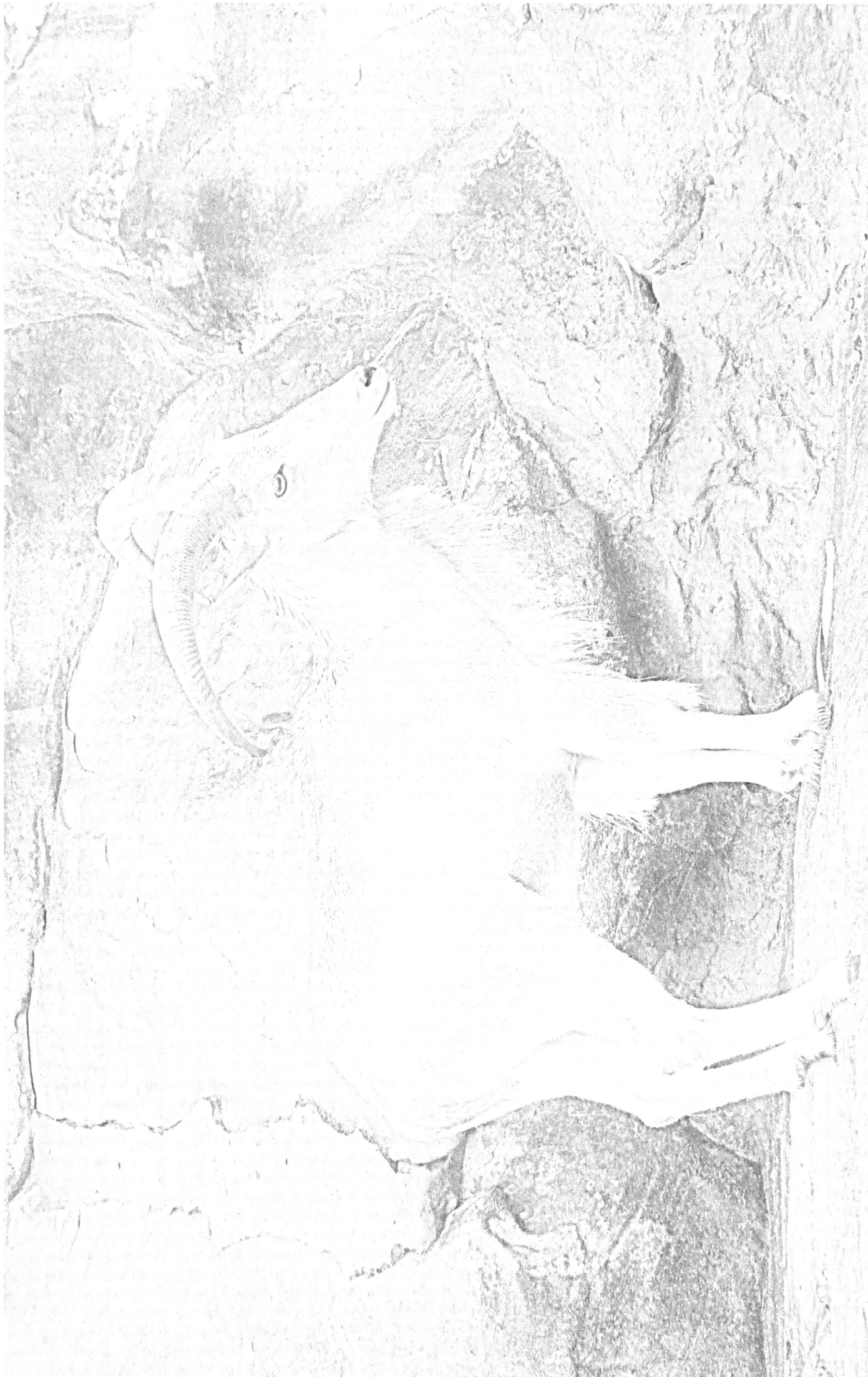

Silo

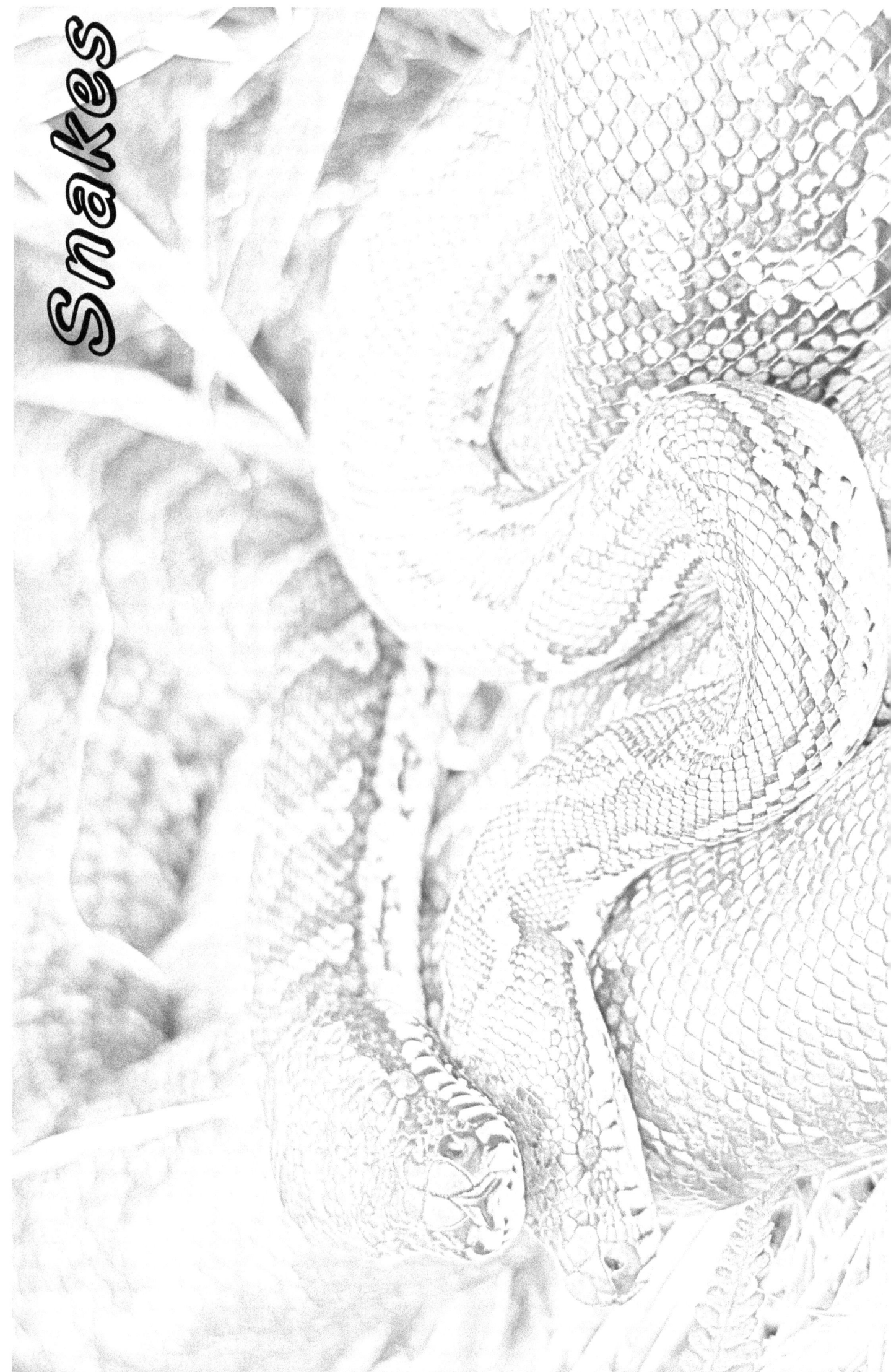

Snakes

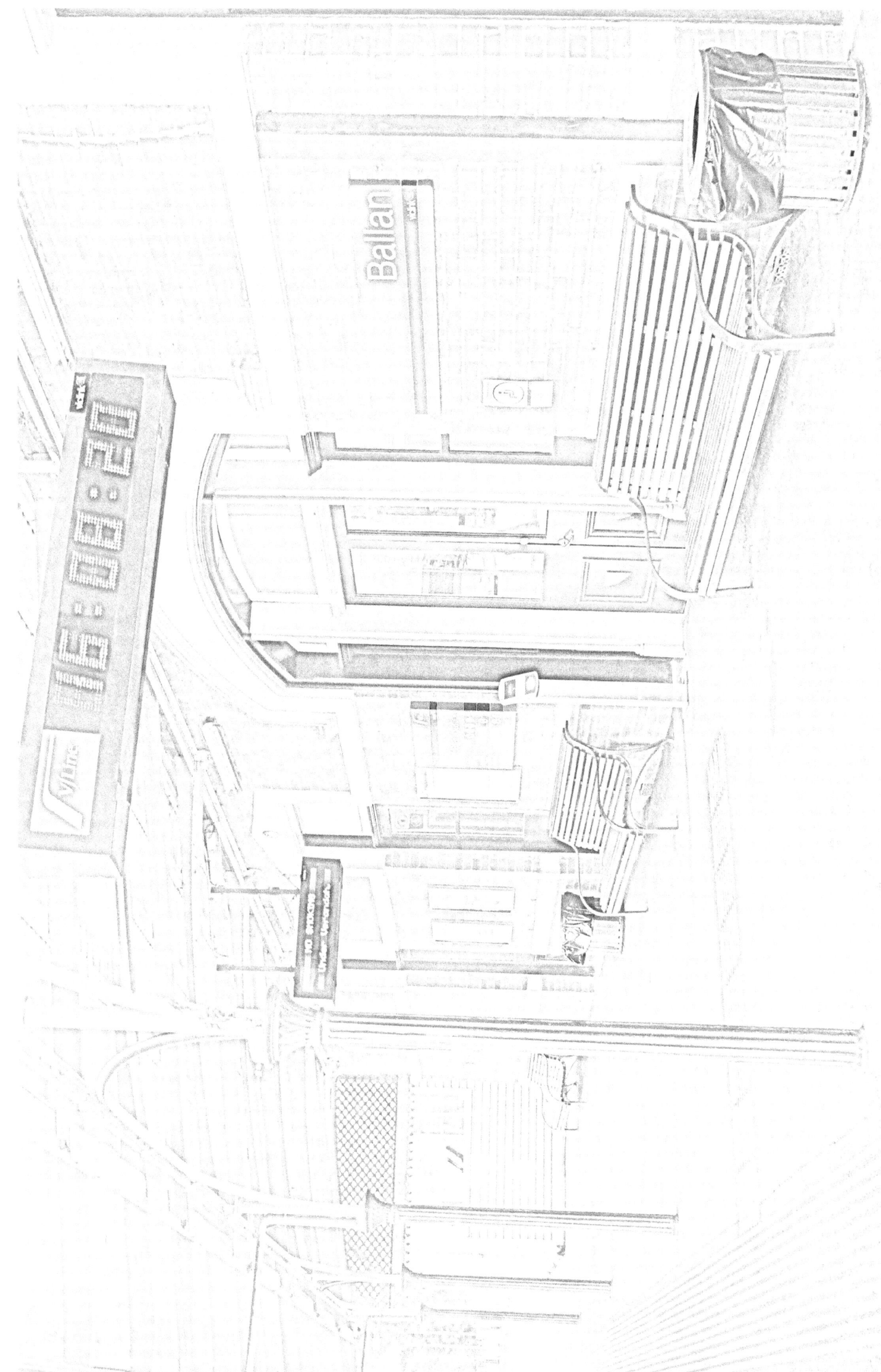

Rusty The Tin Dog

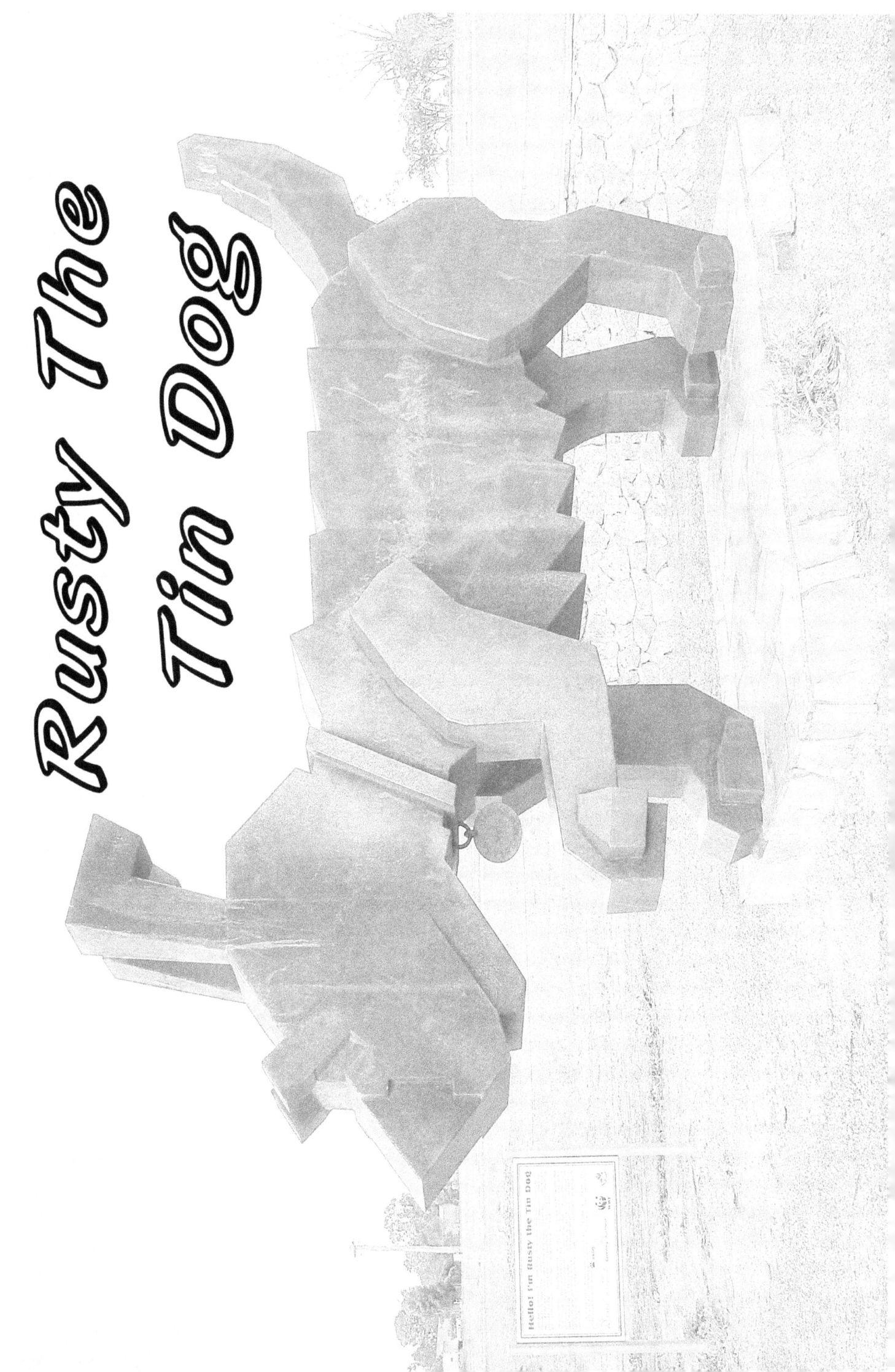

Hello! I'm Rusty the Tin Dog!

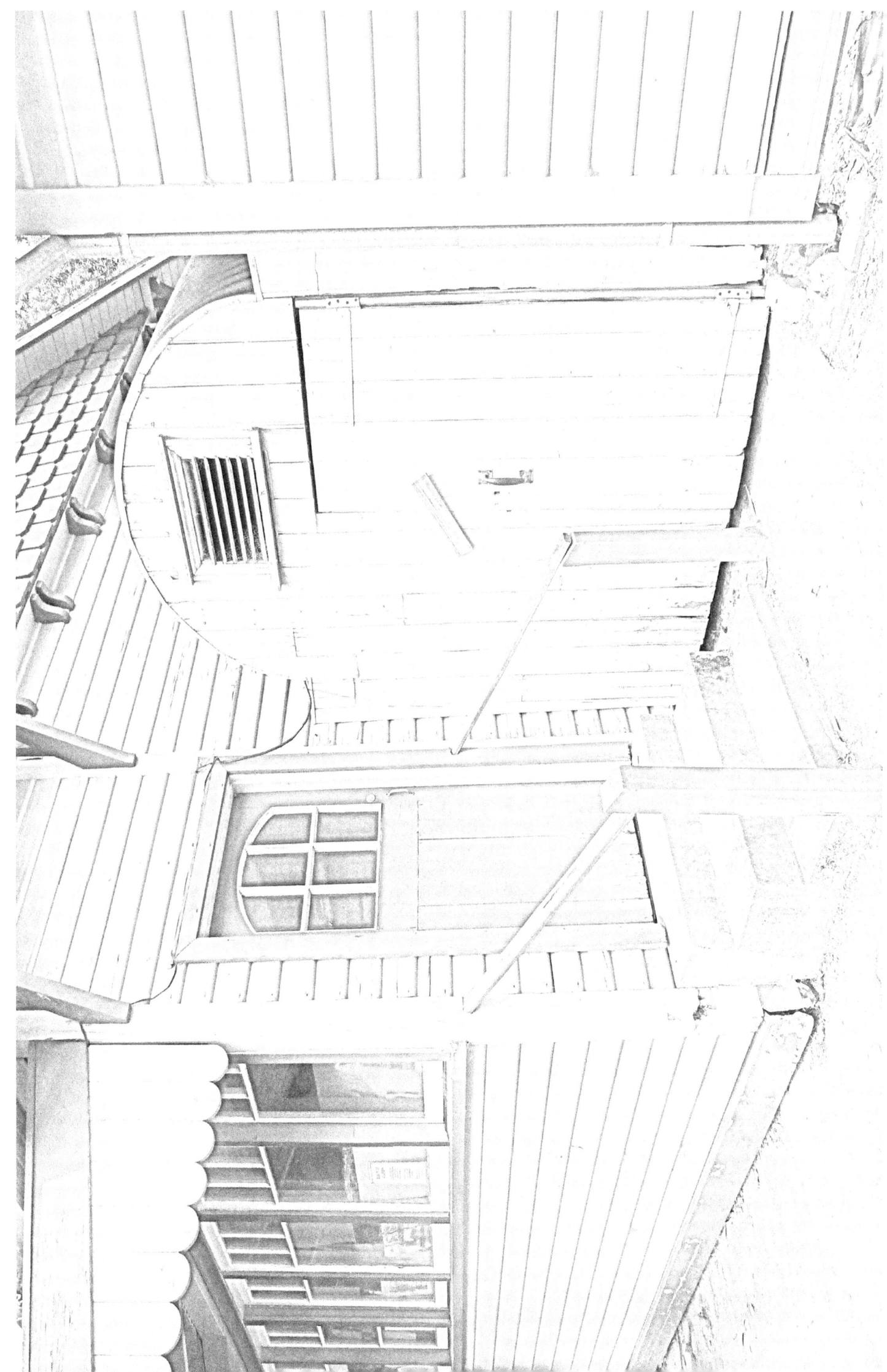

Steam Train

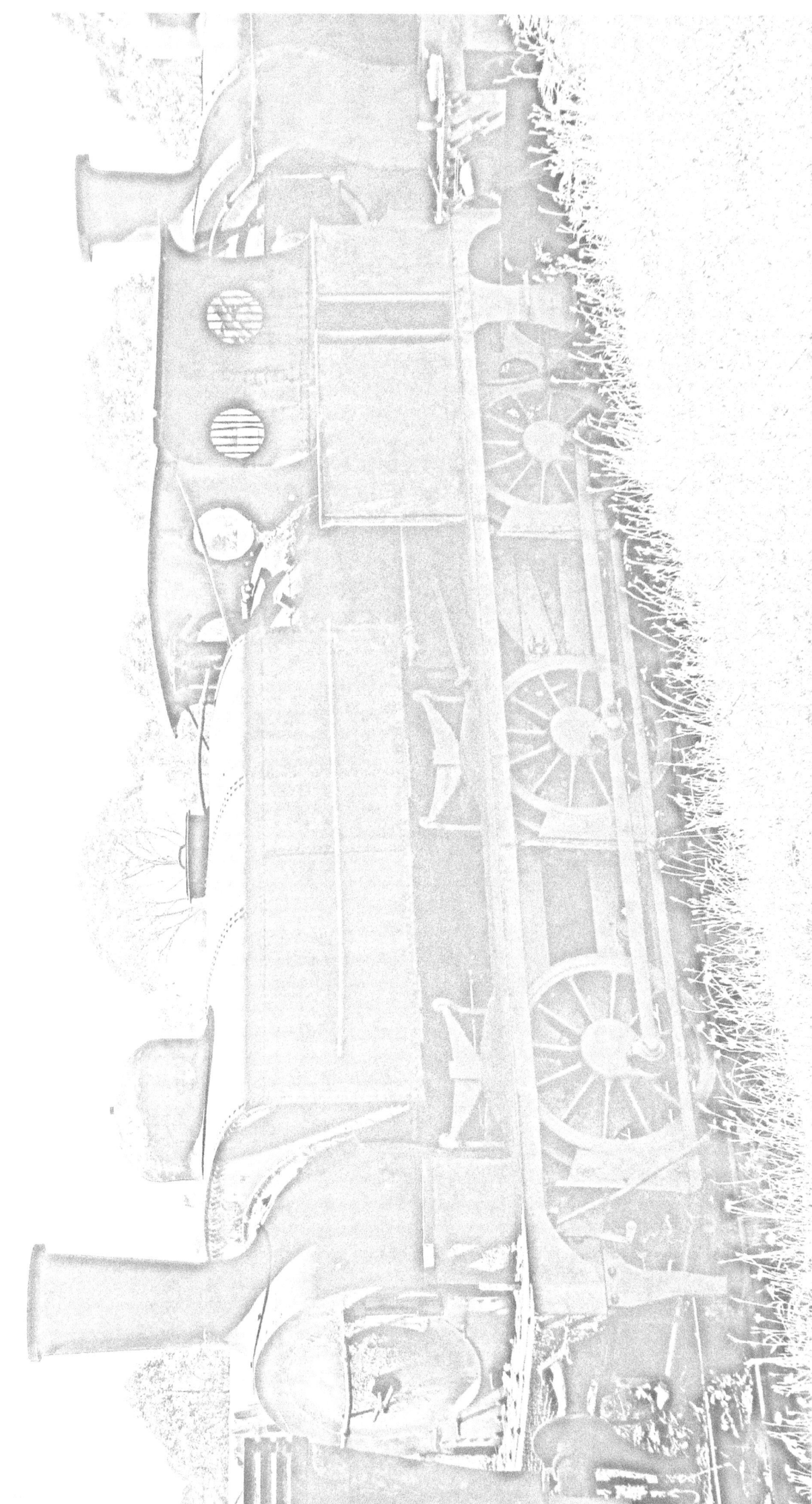

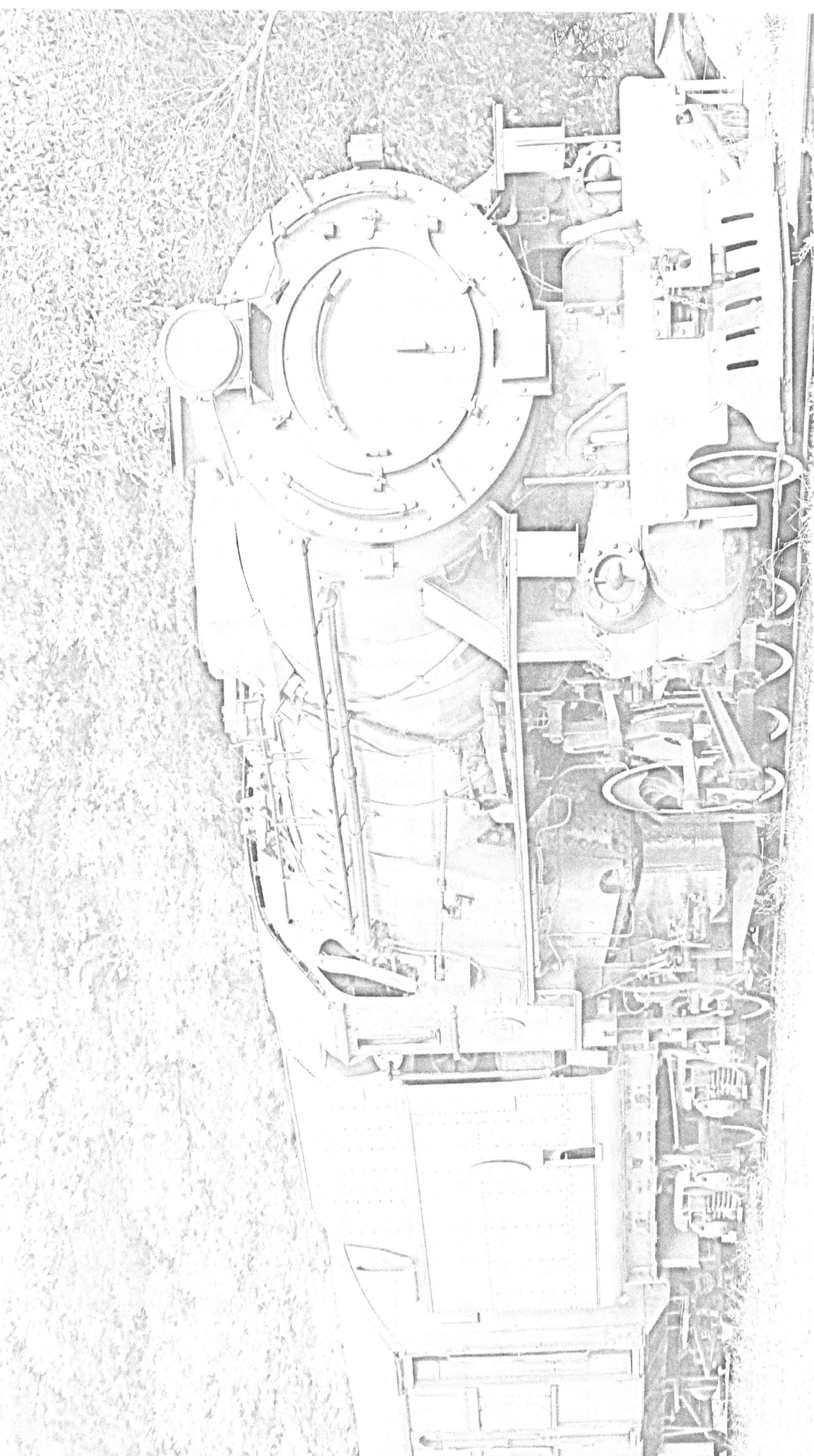

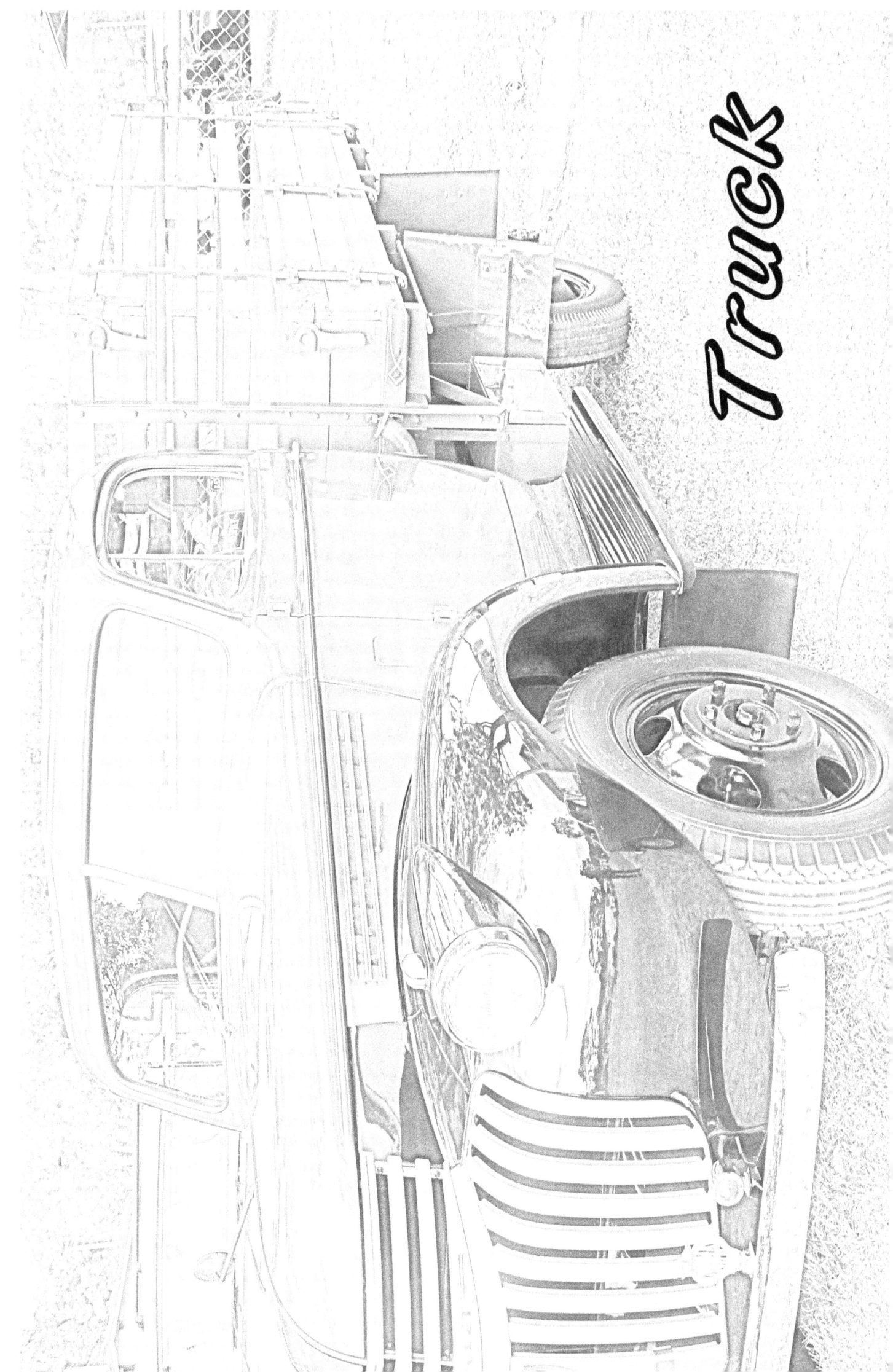

Truck

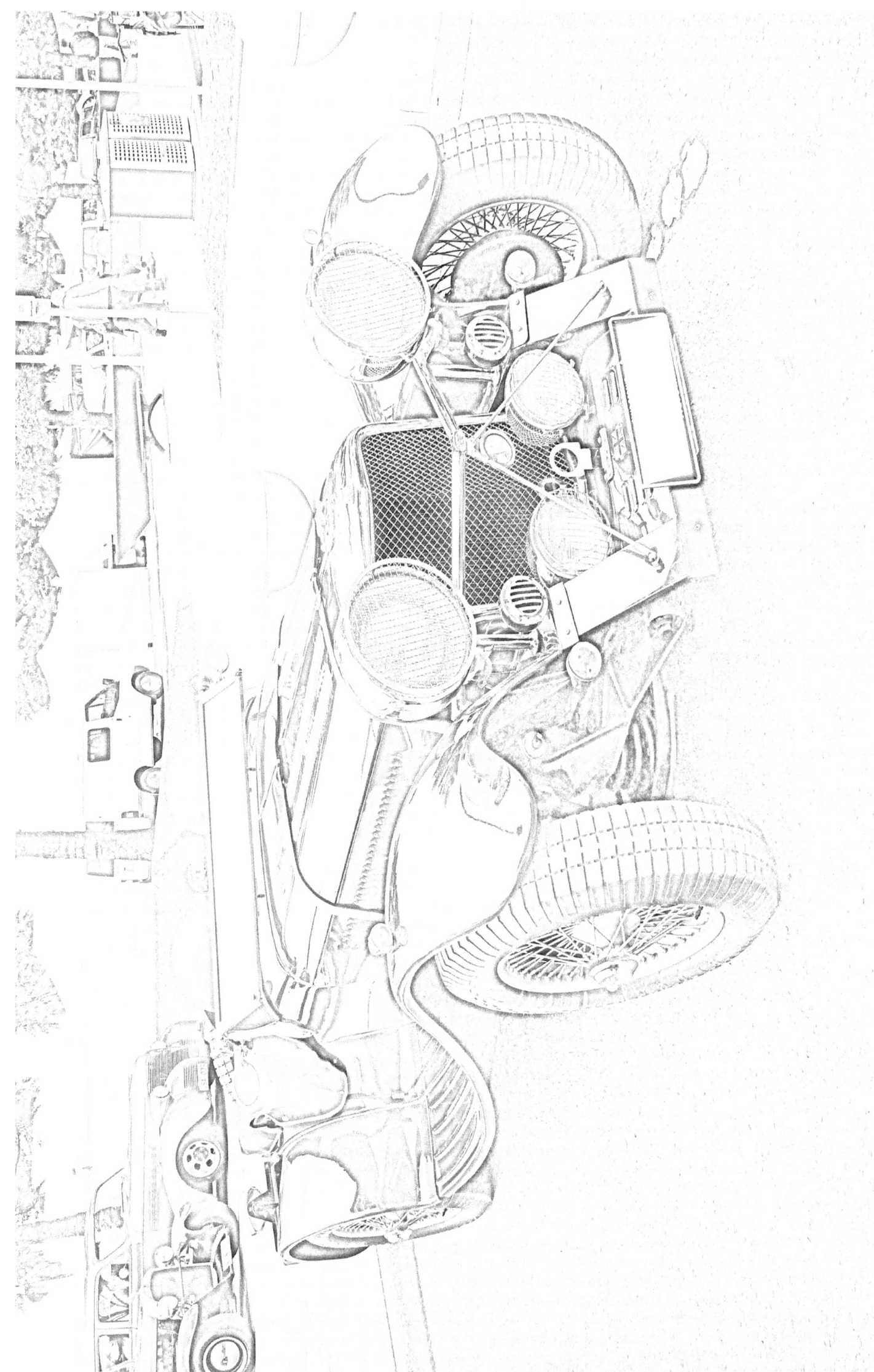

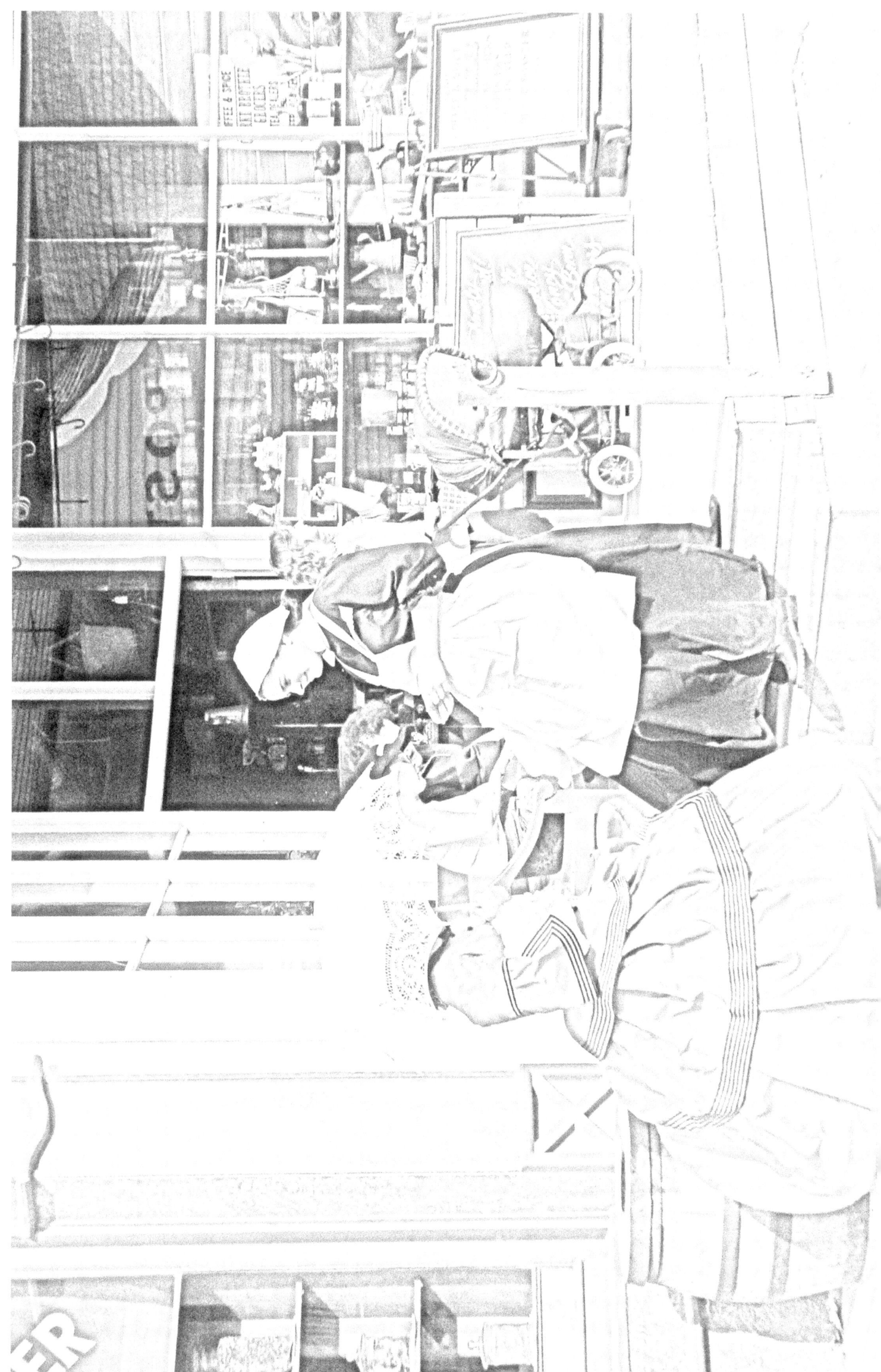

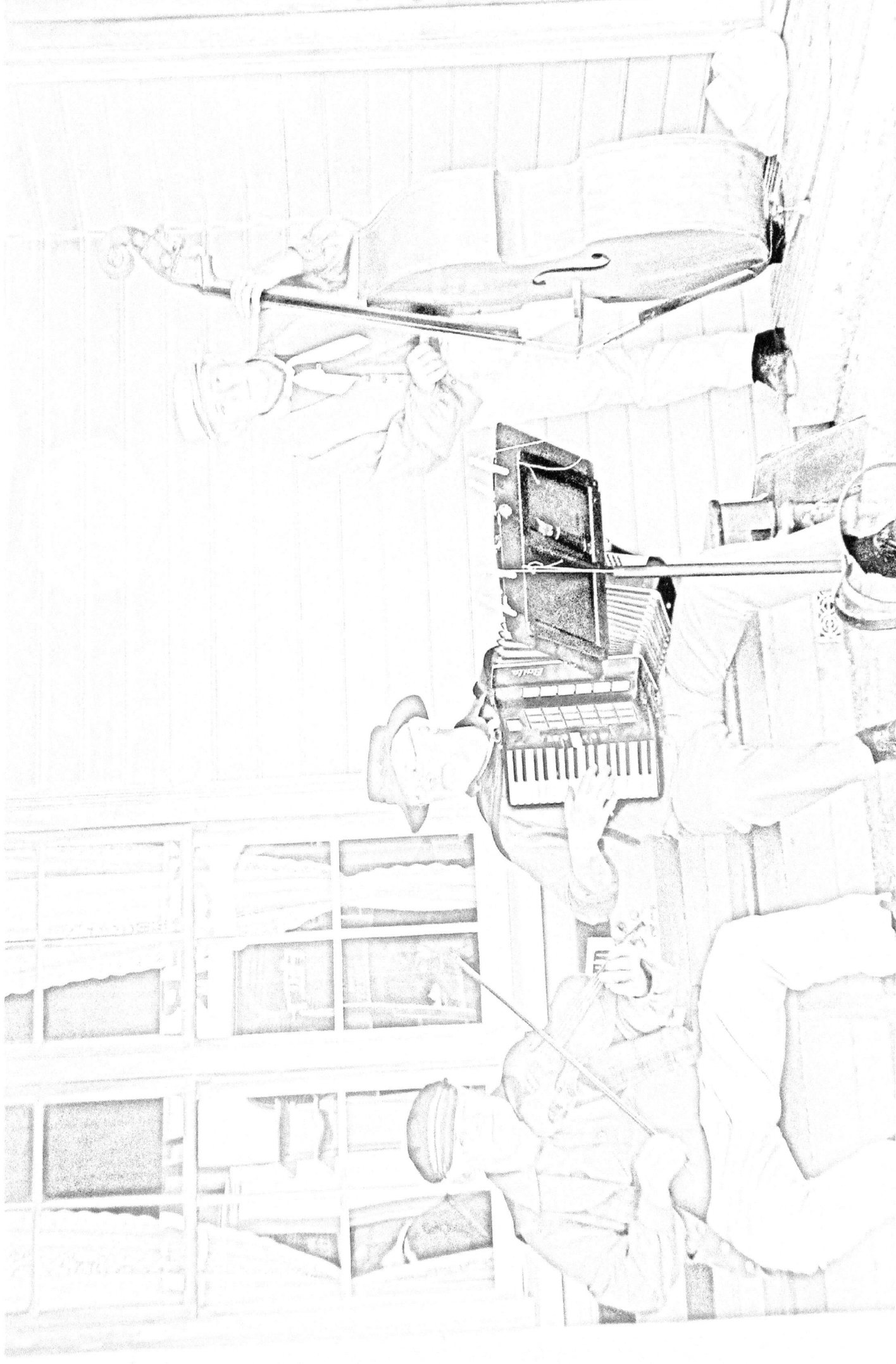

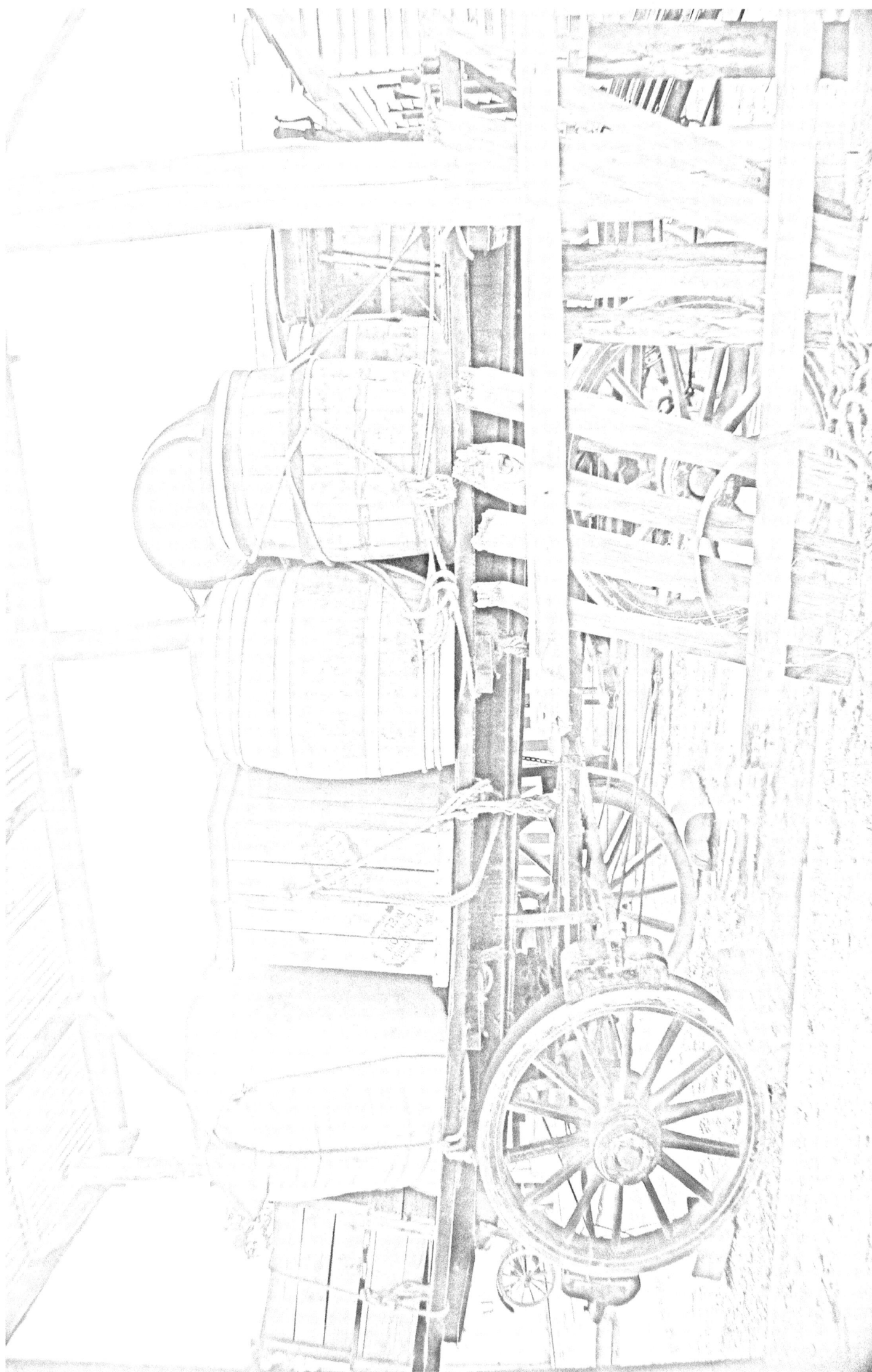

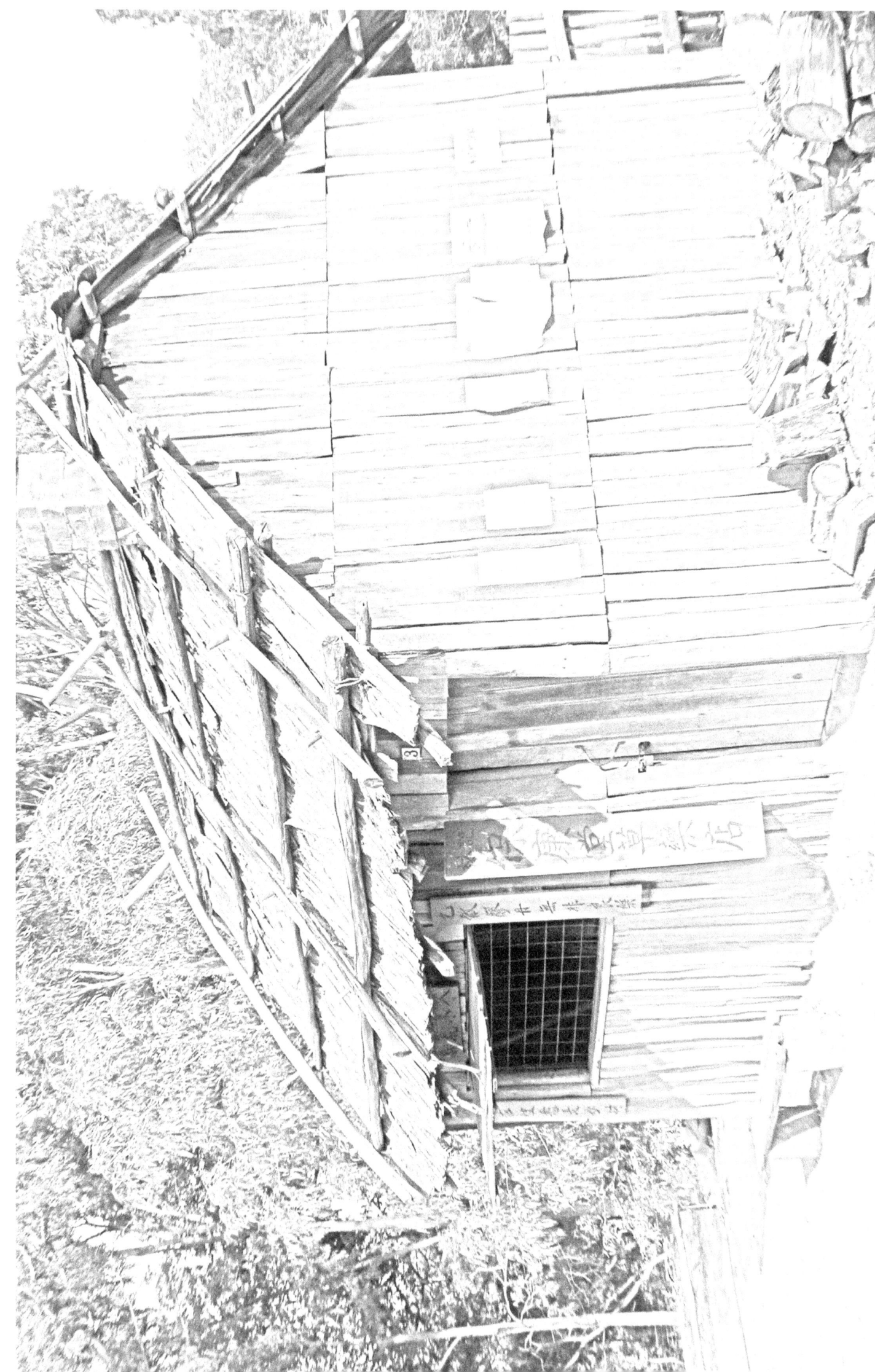

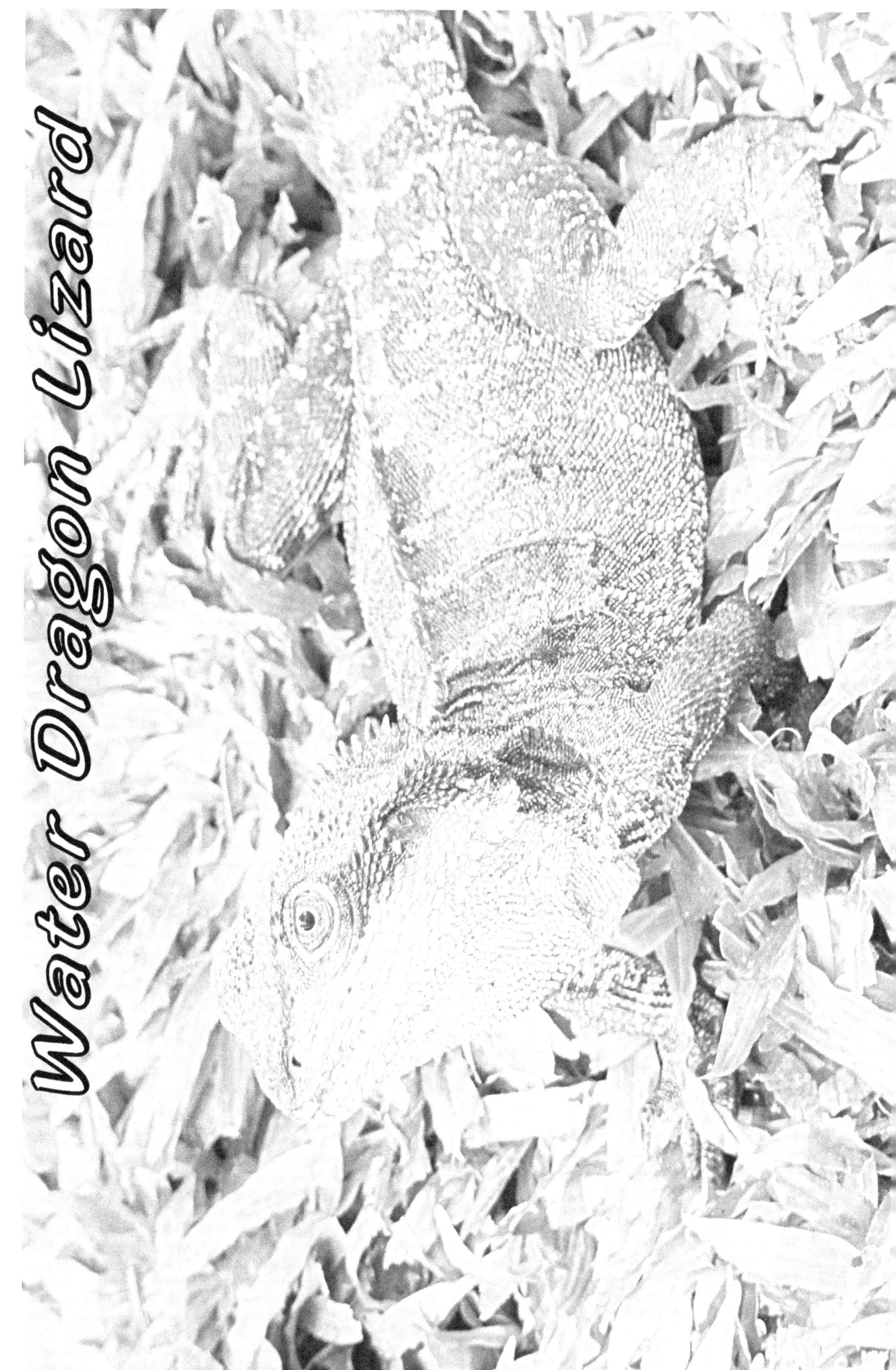

Water Dragon Lizard

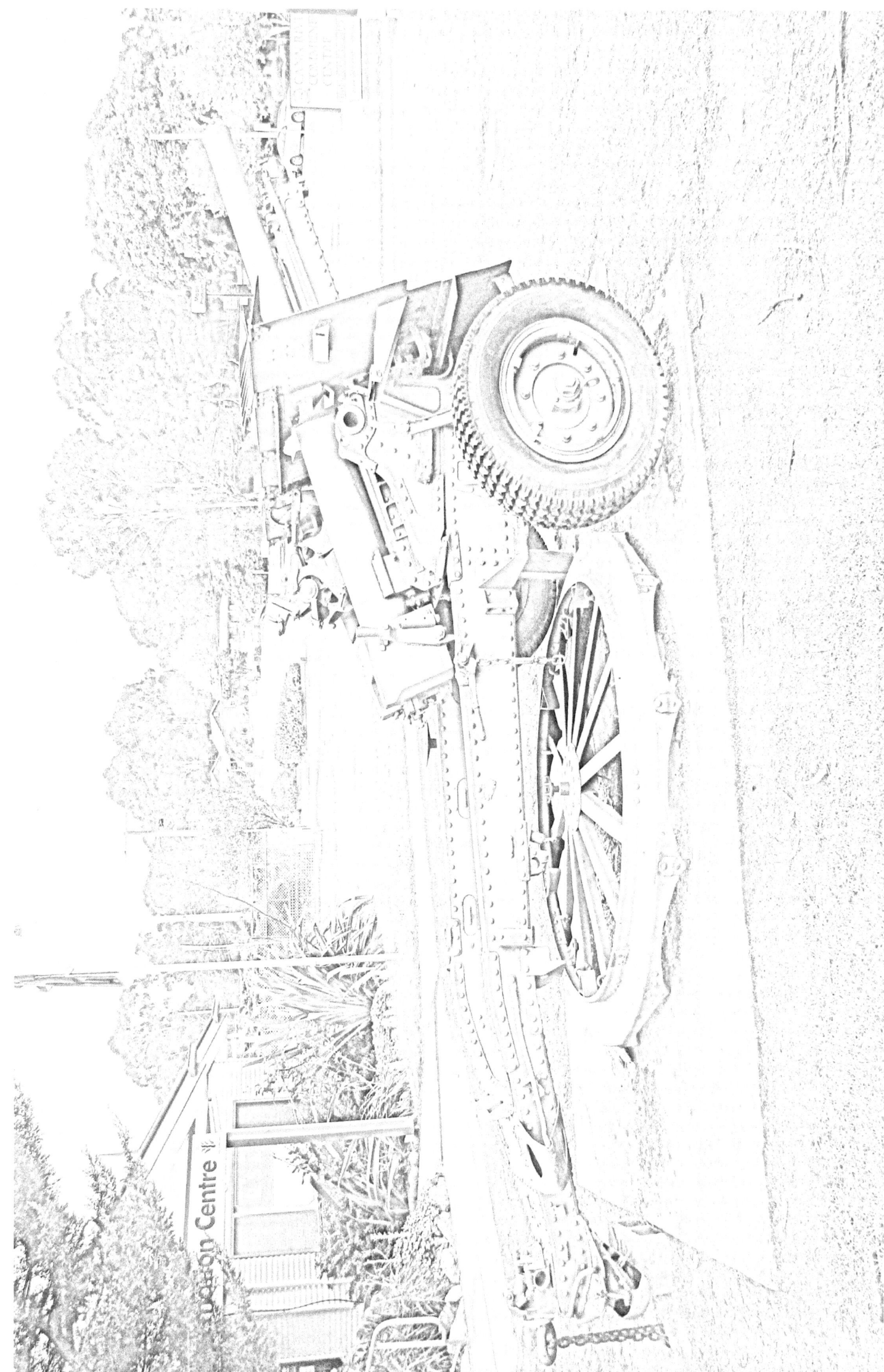

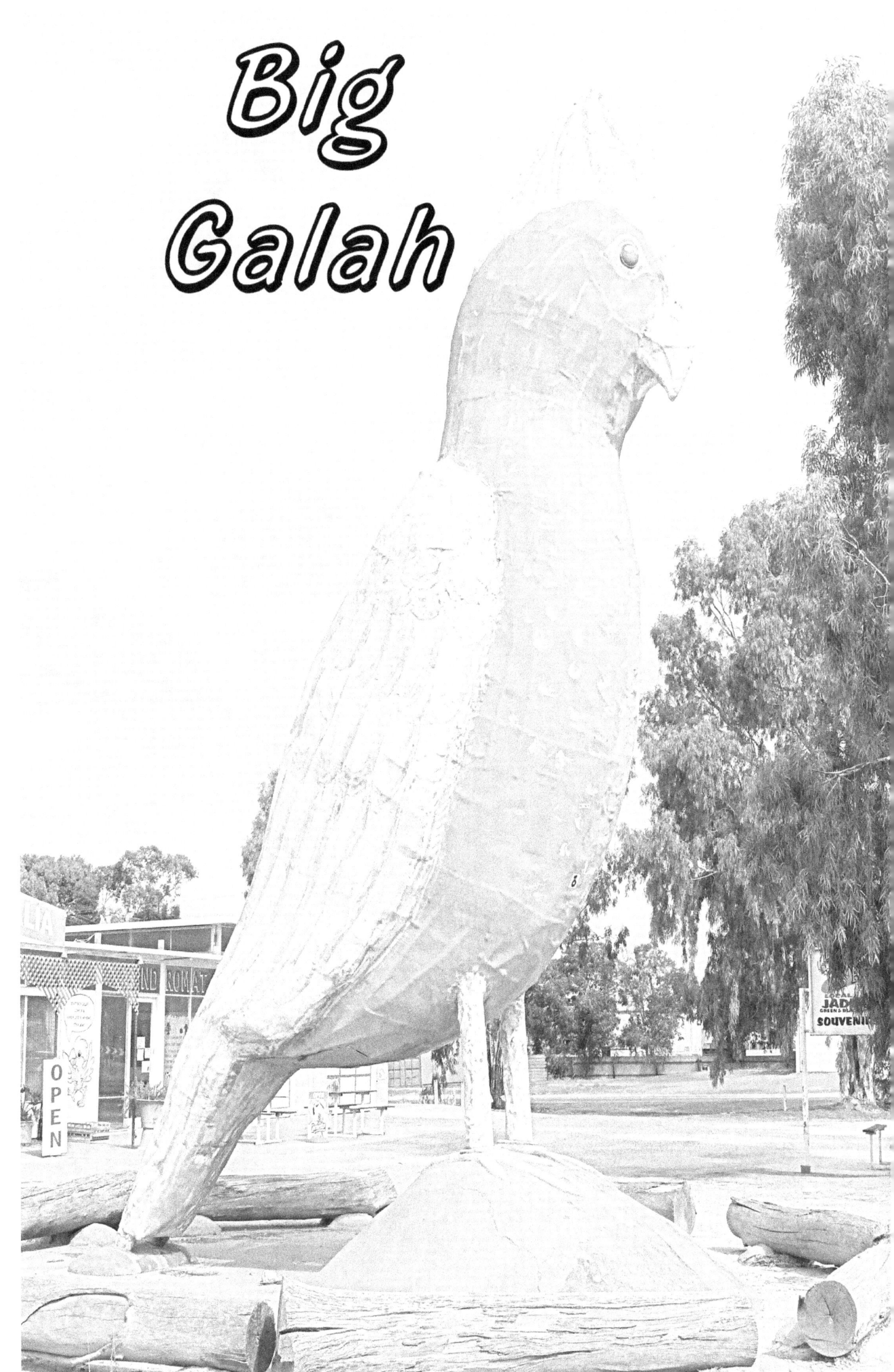

Big
Galah

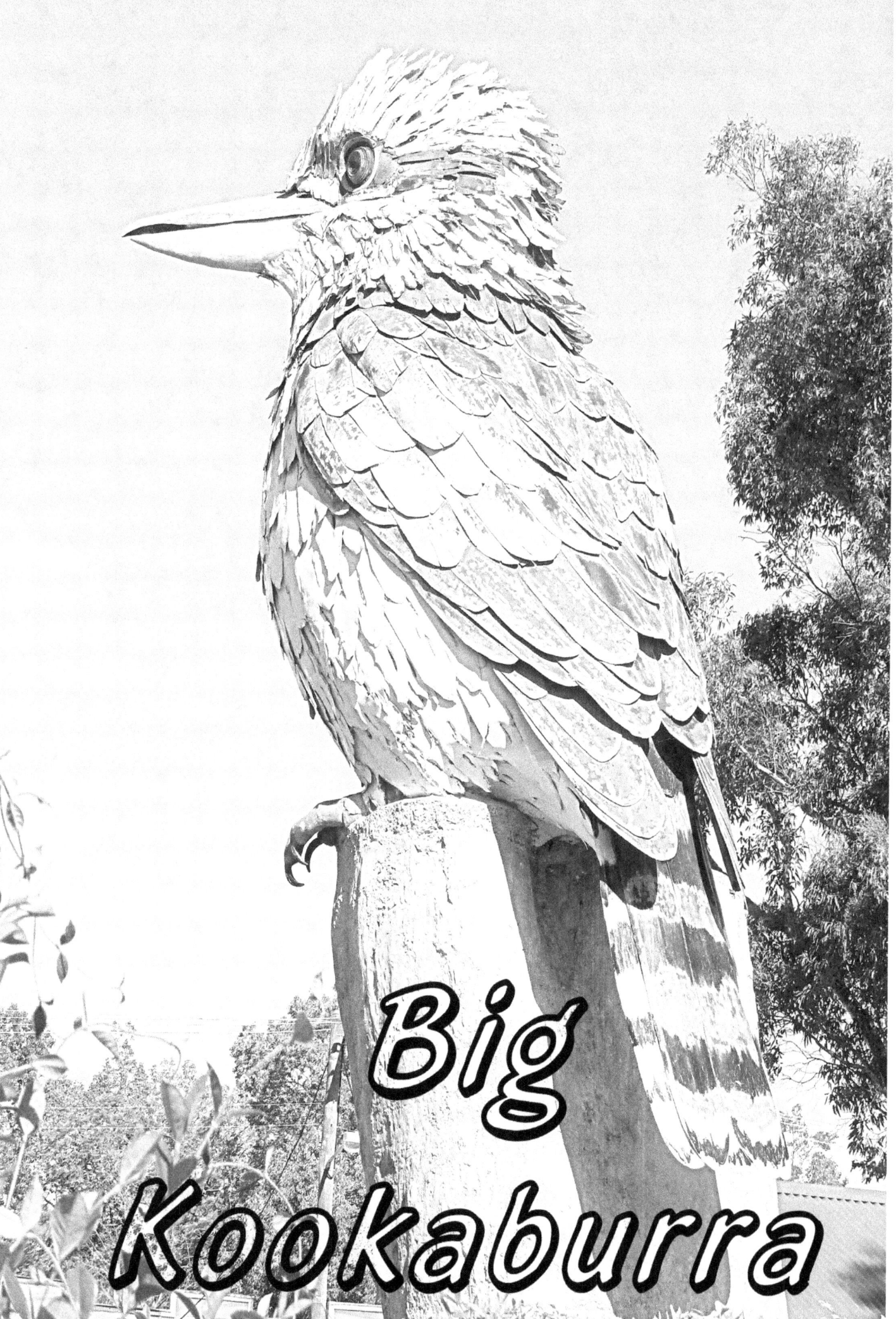

Big
Kookaburra

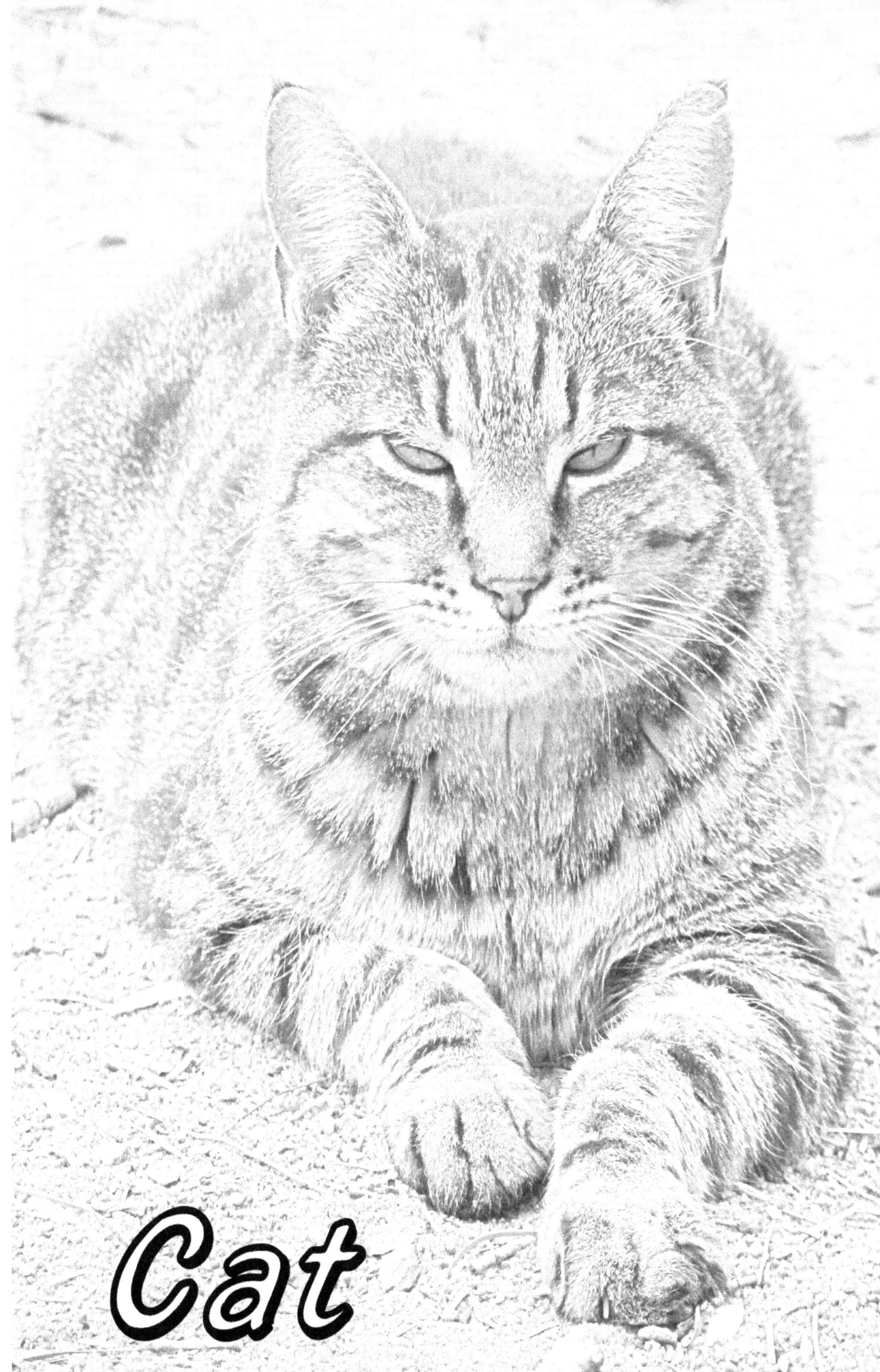

Cat

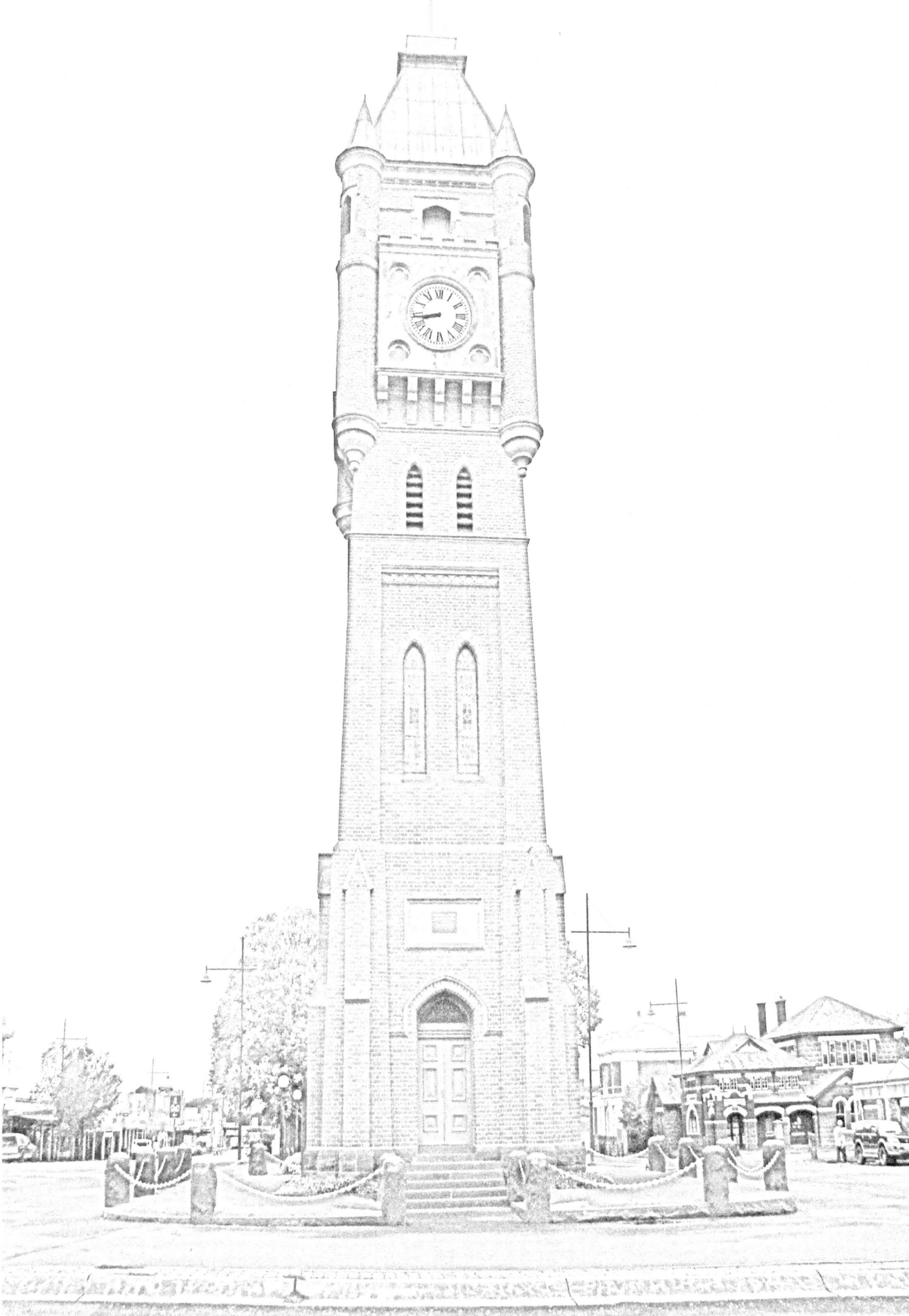

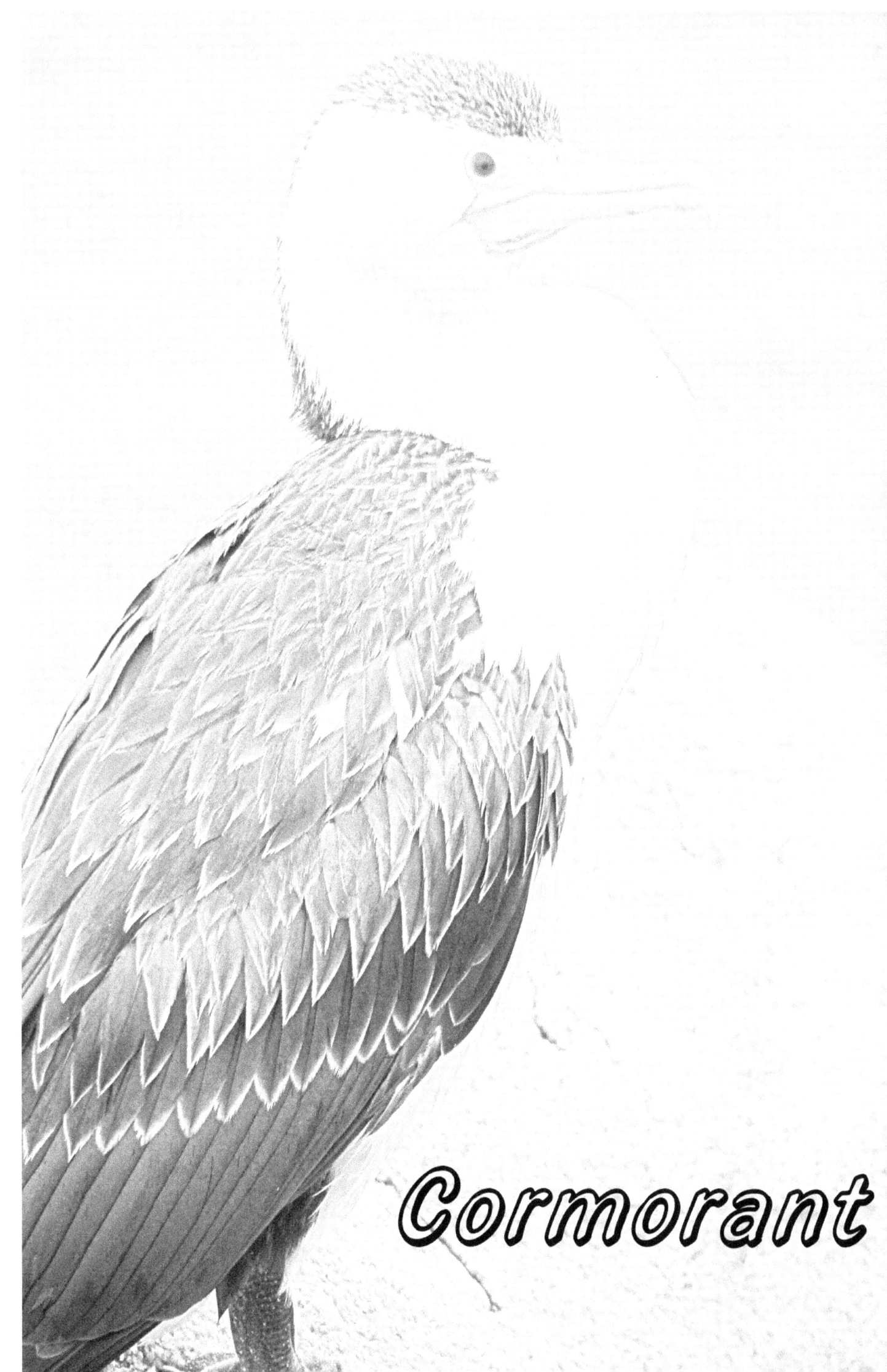

Cormorant

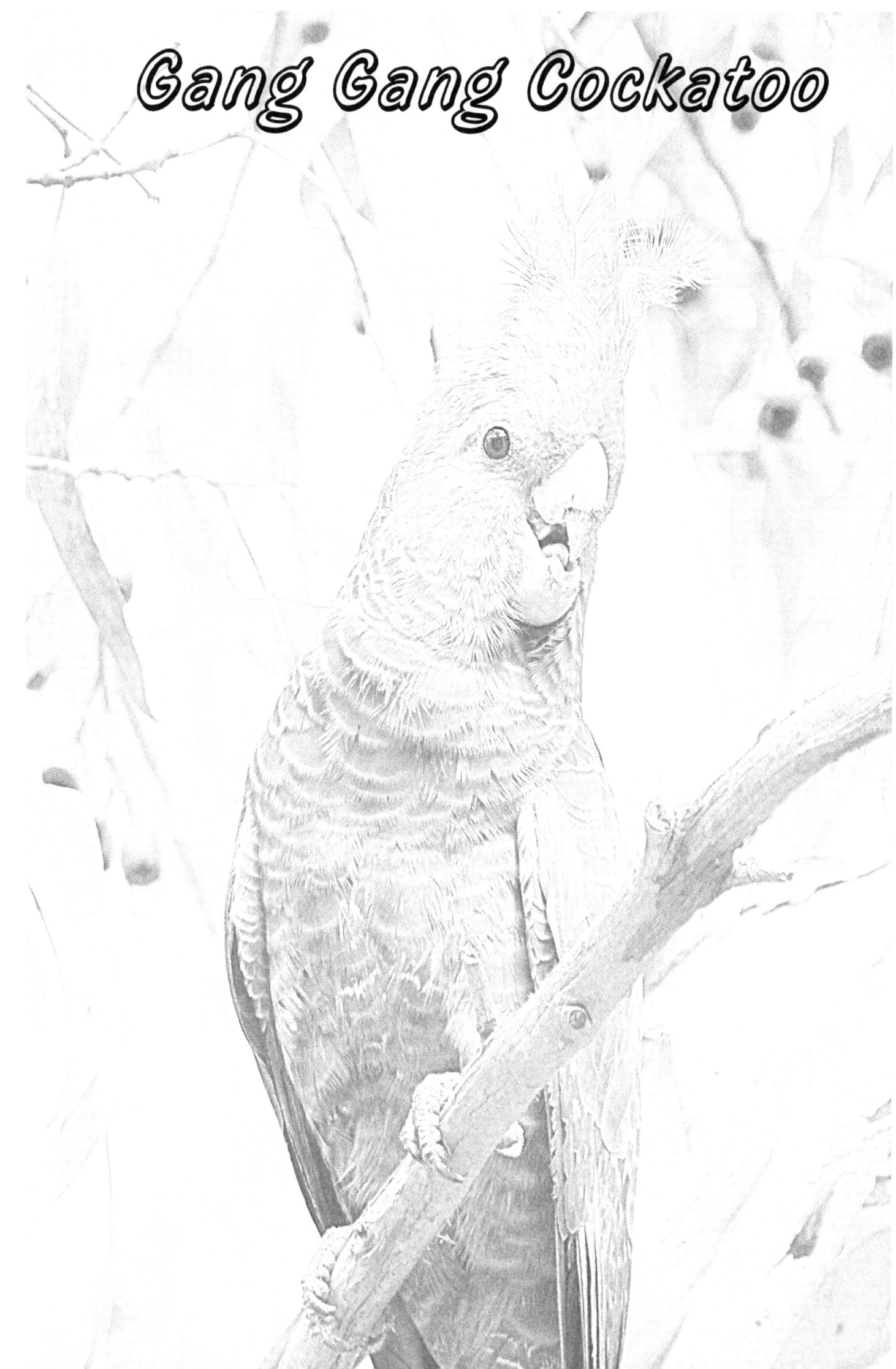

Gang Gang Cockatoo

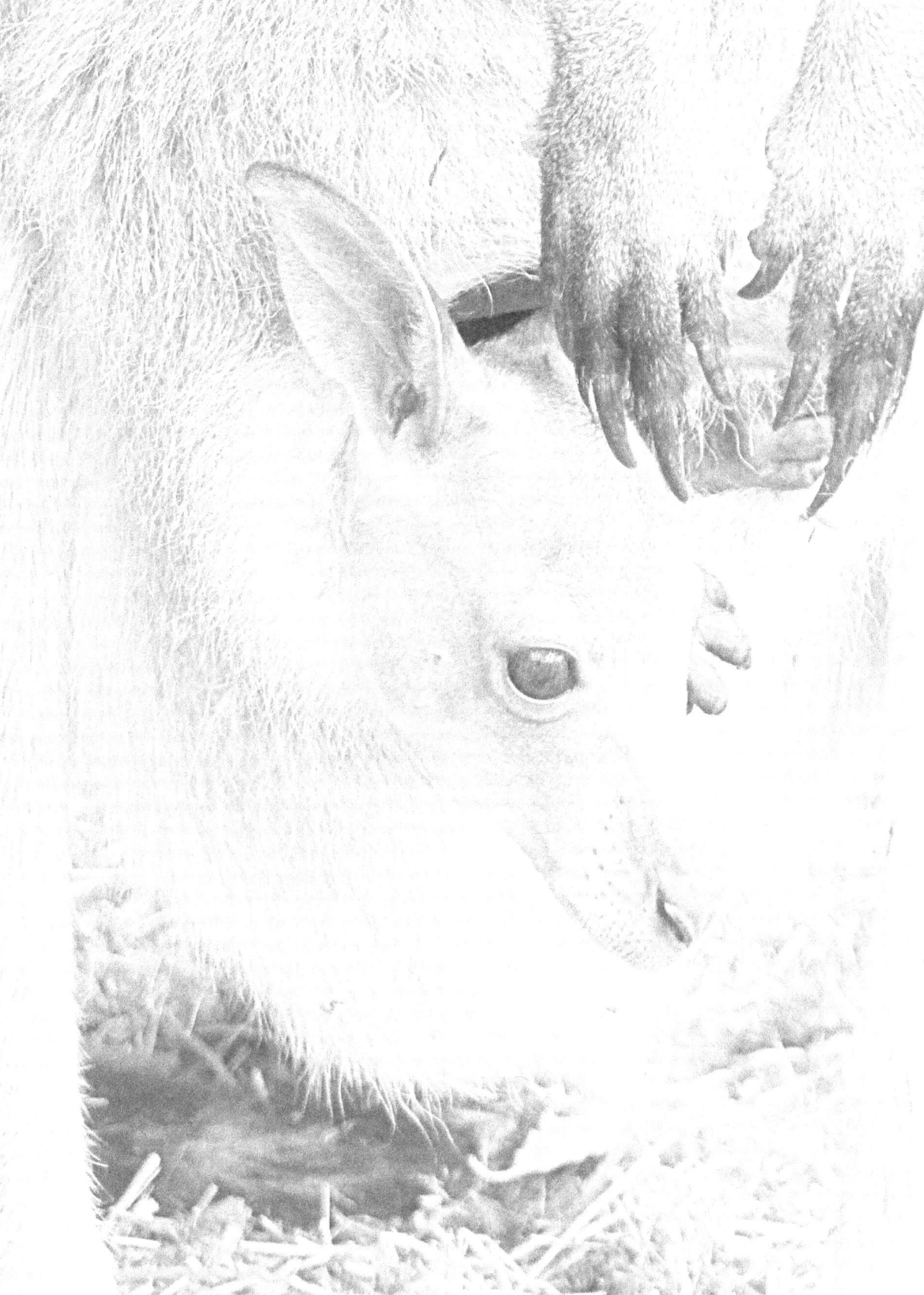

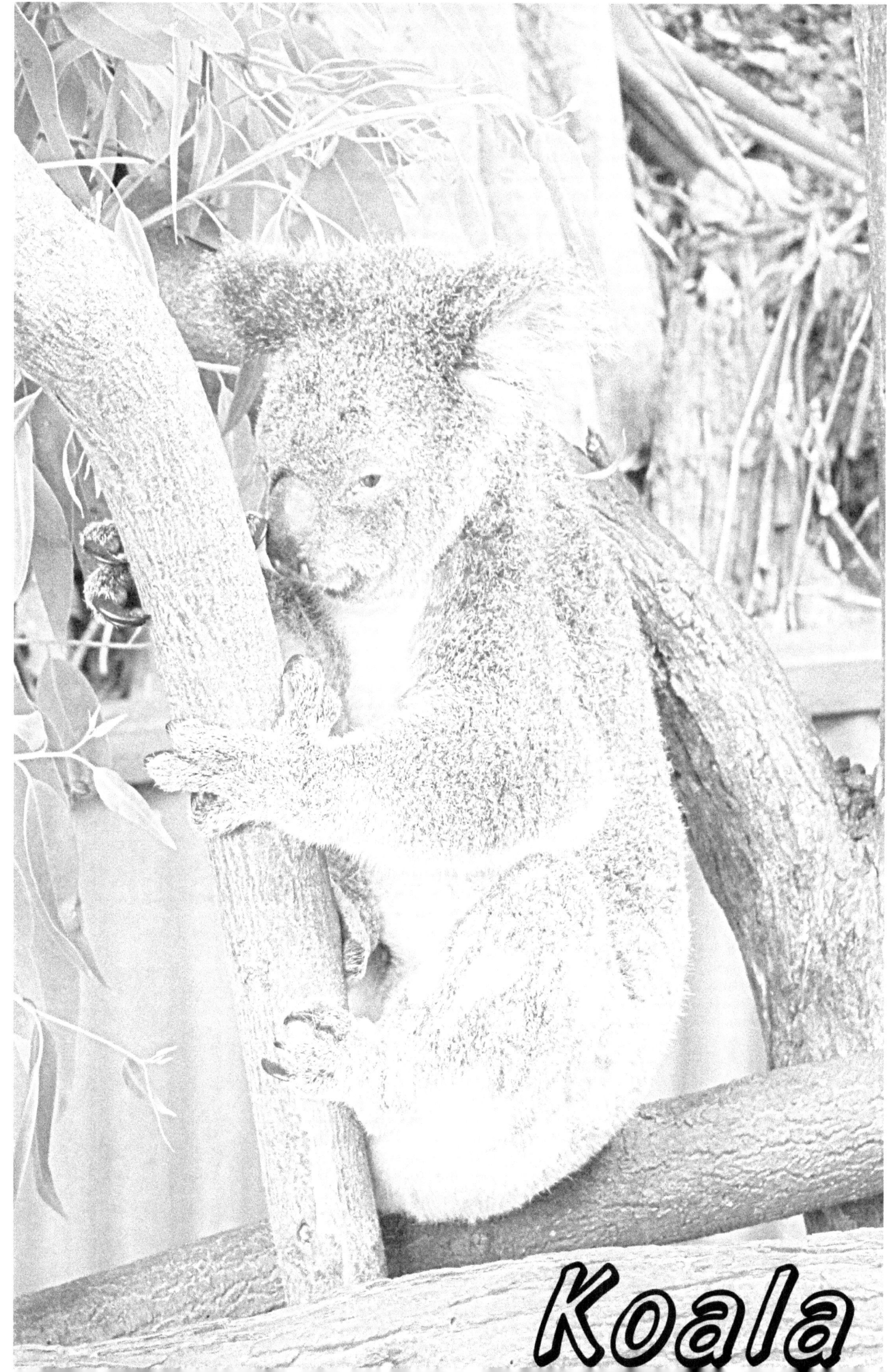

Koala

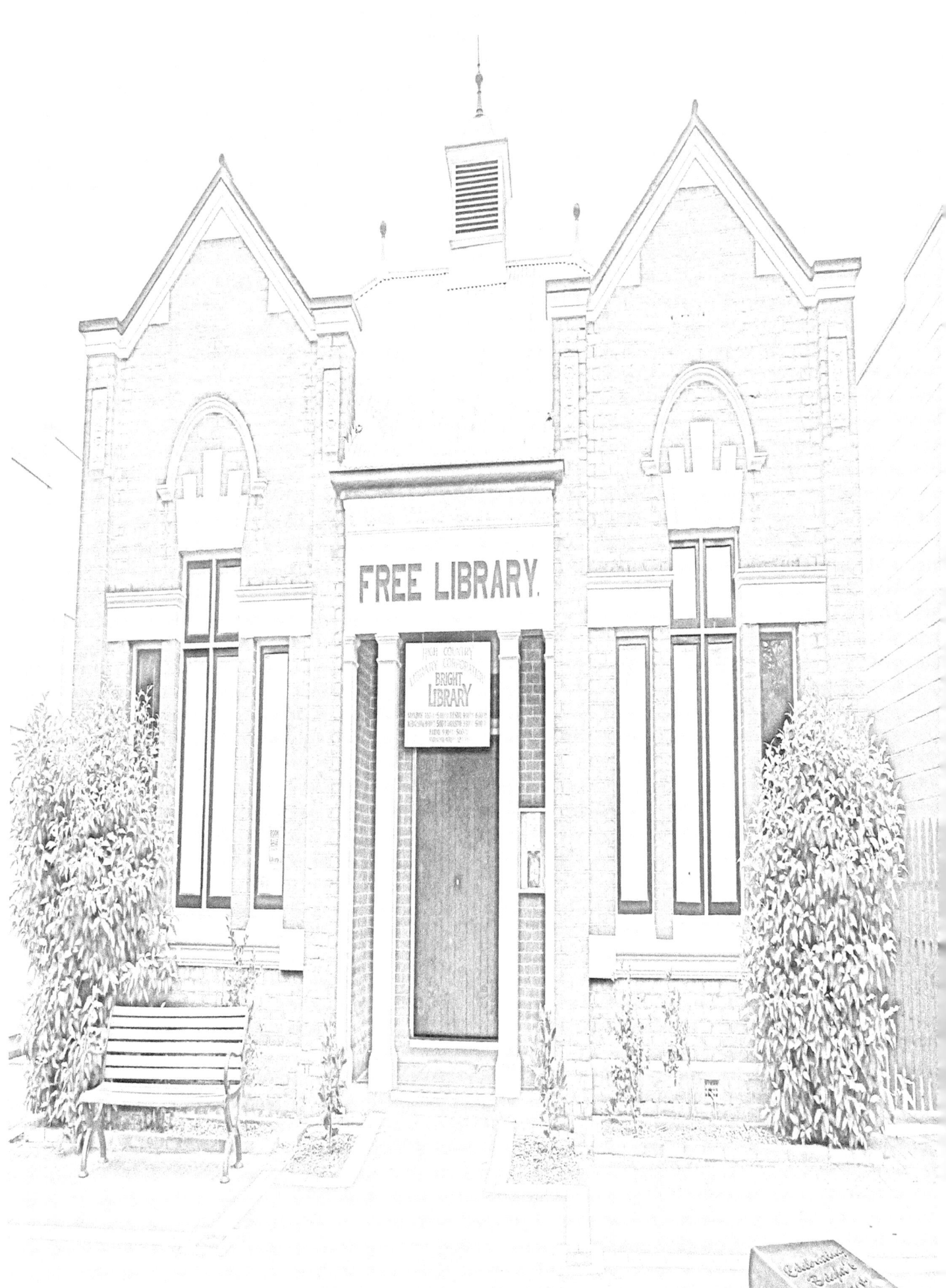

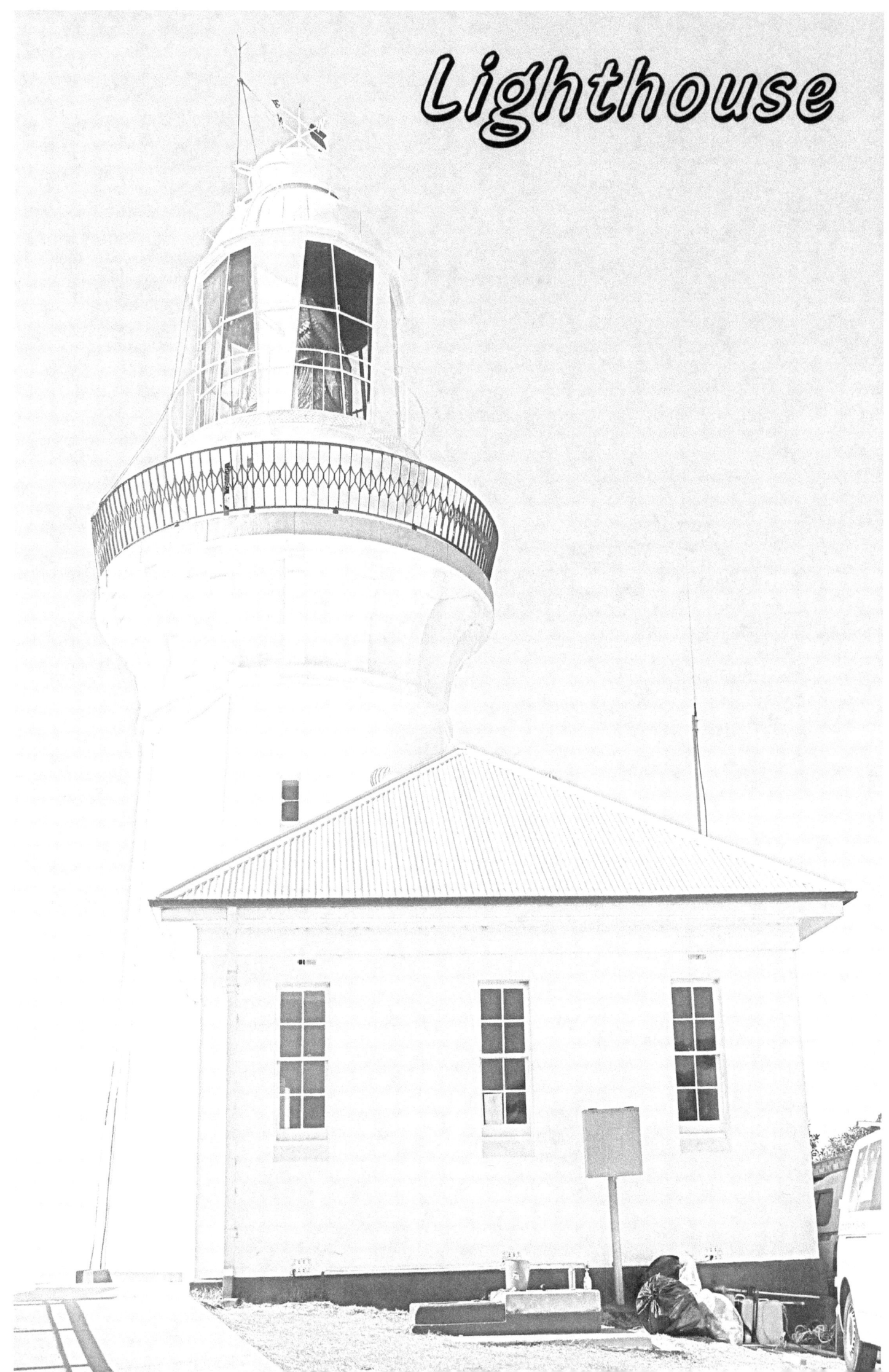

Lighthouse

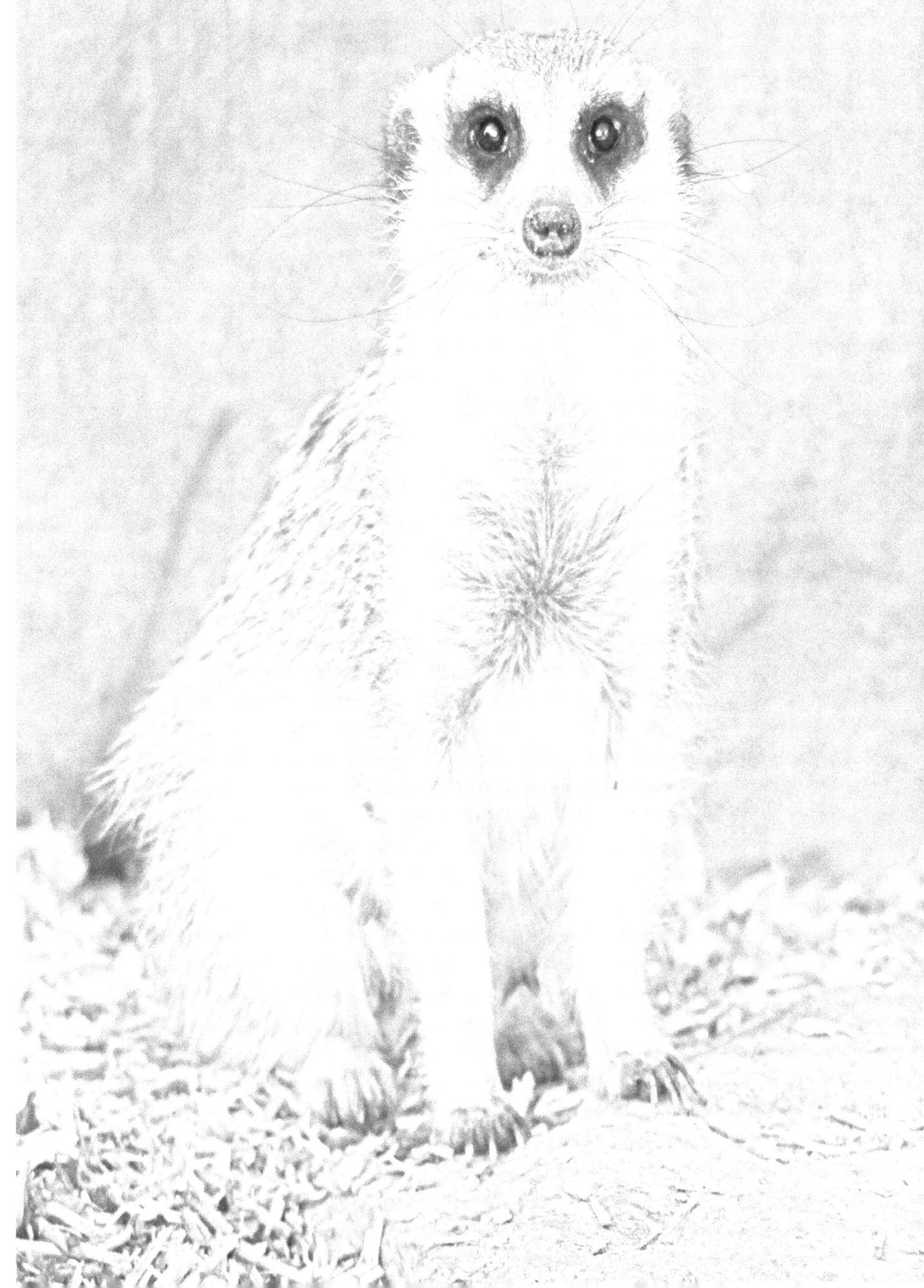

Meerkat

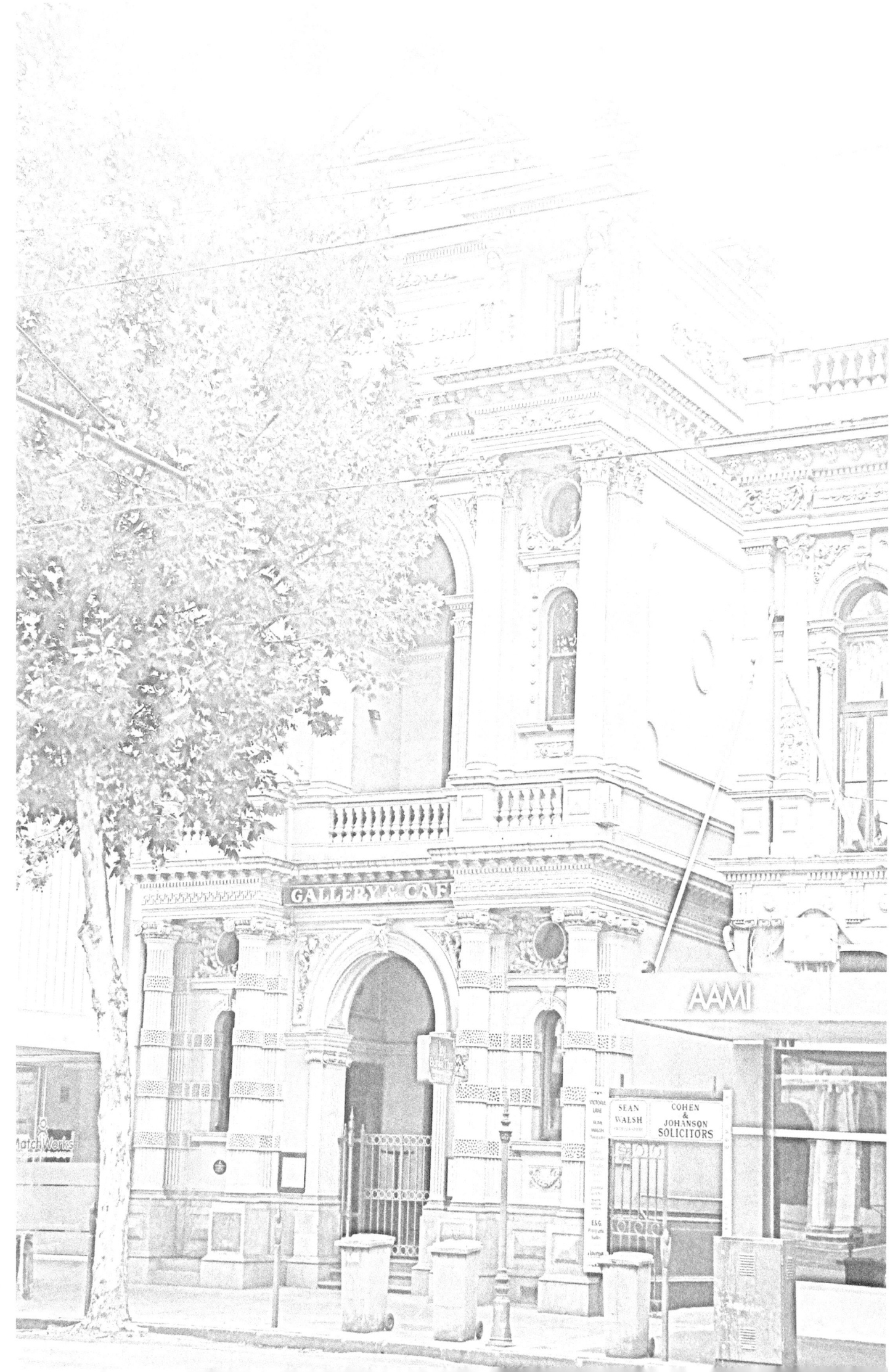

www.ingramcontent.com/pod-product-compliance
Lightning Source LLC
Chambersburg PA
CBHW081048180526
45170CB00005B/1735